Pitseolak

David F. Raine

Pitseolak
A Canadian Tragedy

Hurtig Publishers
Edmonton

Hurtig Publishers Ltd.
10560 - 105 Street
Edmonton, Alberta

Canadian Cataloguing in Publication Data

Raine, David F., 1941-
   Pitseolak, a Canadian tragedy

   ISBN 0-88830-186-3

   1. Pitseolak, 1945-1969   2. Inuit —
Northwest Territories — Biography.   I. Title.
FC4173.1.P5R3   971.9'2'00994   C80-091008-7
F1060.92.P5R3

Maps by Jill Amos Raine
Typeset by Pickering Type House
Manufactured by T. H. Best Printing Company Ltd.

For Eetusajuk
so that she may better understand her childhood

For Pitseolak
her uncle, so that all was not in vain

Preface

Pitseolak was twenty-three when I met him. Seven short months later he would be dead, although at the time there was no reason for either of us to suspect it.

I can see now that he was somehow destined to be caught in this morbid web, the strands of which we began to weave that day of our first meeting. But, even now, knowing what I do, I would not have helped Pitseolak to spin a different fabric. Neither of us would or, indeed, could have done so. We both knew that he was already ensnared by a cultural conflict from which he could not escape.

In a sense, this is the story of a brief friendship, but it is also an account of the circumstances that led to the inevitable and tragic death of a young Eskimo, somewhere in the icy wastes of the tundra.

The story presented here is true. Perhaps that in itself is a Canadian tragedy.

Acknowledgements

I would like to thank the following people who have contributed to the preparation of this book: Ted Simpkins, who listened to the initial outline of the text and first understood the significance of Pitseolak; Pamela Adory, whose questioning interest has helped me with my thinking and who also undertook the editing and typing of the final draft, for which I am most grateful; and Mangitak, who taught me so much about his culture and whose family offered me warmth in the cold.

I also wish to offer a collective thanks to the people of Cape Dorset, Baffin Island. By enabling me to experience their lives, they have given me an indelible perspective on my own.

David F. Raine

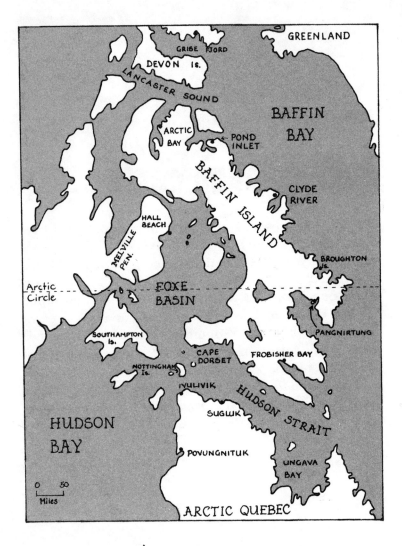

CANADA'S EASTERN ARCTIC

One

I watched him running towards me. From the comfort of my armchair I could see him clearly, his face wrinkled into that of an older man as icy gusts of arctic air blasted at his skin.

He almost jogged towards the house, eyes darting busily as he took care to avoid the treacherous snowdrifts. Each time he exhaled, tiny particles of breath seemed to freeze instantly onto the dog-fur trimming around the edge of his hood. Looking at him through the snow-spattered window, I thought how typically Inuit he was, complete with thigh-length parka and caribou mittens. Yet even then I was aware that he was somehow different from the others in this remote tundra settlement — perhaps because of his uncertain gait or maybe because of his corduroy trousers and lace-up rubber boots.

I put down the outdated newspaper I had been reading, and as I did so I heard his feet on the steps outside. A couple of dull thuds, a gentle kick against the prefabricated plywood walls of the house, and I knew that he was inside the first pair of doors. Then there were the predictable sounds as he stood in the outer entrance slipping off his hood, dusting the snow from his clothing, and stamping his boots free of icy slush. The second pair of doors burst open, and he was in the room, stripping off his outdoor clothing and bounding forward with the excited air of someone who hopes he isn't late for an important supper party. "Hi," he said with a broad smile.

He took a plastic comb from his back pocket and quickly groomed his hair into the well-greased style of the 1950s — sides swept sharply backwards into a dovetail somewhere in the rear; with an abrupt flick of experience, a quiff rose immaculately above his forehead.

"It's cold outside!" He offered a friendly laugh and advanced across the carpeting to shake my hand. "My name is Pitseolak," he announced with pride, "Pit-choo-la," repeating the word slowly and phonetically so that I would forever say it correctly. But he also pronounced it with firmness, as if he wanted to leave it deliberately and indelibly impressed on my mind.

We shook hands, and even before I could suggest it, he made himself comfortable in the nearest armchair, his head enthusiastically turning in all directions as he blatantly absorbed the furnishings and decor with an inquisitive and approving eye. His general manner was rather like that of a remote relative who has decided to invite himself for a six-month holiday, or perhaps that of a friendly tax man who has come to assess one's wealth over a cup of coffee.

The house was indeed delightful, even luxurious: two bedrooms, a study, dining area, modern kitchen, and sunken living room. It had wall-to-wall carpeting, double glazing, and central heating. There were teak furnishings, coffee tables, and elegant drapes flanking the windows. My wife and I had at first been rather embarrassed by so many comforts, for our home bore all the trademarks of status and wealth, contrasting strongly with the sparsely decorated dwellings of our Inuit neighbours. "How do you feel," I had asked one of them guiltily, "sitting in my house, with all of its comforts, when your own home is so bleak and stark?" He had grinned. "You need it," he had said. "We don't." His attitude lent a satisfying perspective that I could at least live with. A different form of comfort: reality.

So I felt only curiosity as I stood looking at this exuberant youth who seemed so much at home in my favourite chair. He exuded a confidence and familiarity that would have suggested to a bystander that we were longtime friends. In fact, this was the first time we had met and only the second time I had even seen him.

He sat comfortably, nestling into the cushion, briskly rubbing the palms of his hands, eyes roaming from ceiling to floor, from bookcase to radio, and from corner to corner. His appearance was an absurd deviation from the local norm, in fact "distinctive" anywhere: a peculiar flecked shirt, held fast at the collar by a flamboyant tie that suddenly widened at the bottom; patterned department store socks; brown corduroy trousers neatly pressed to a crease; and a wide leather belt with ends clasped together by a sparkling golden cowboy holding onto a bucking bronco for dear life. With no apparent understanding of the need to co-ordinate a colour scheme, his presentation was both meticulous and preposterous — avant-garde, to say the least. All of this was topped by the strong aroma of after-shave lotion. But his face was warm and friendly, and I liked him instantly, though I knew nothing about him. Maybe this showed.

"I am the brother of Mangitak, and Martha is my sister," he was suddenly saying. "I've just arrived back from Frobisher Bay."

With these random clues, he became totally familiar to me, just like a distant cousin who might arrive at the door and say, "I'm Aunt Clara's boy." In this small Eskimo community of barely five hundred inhabitants, his name and background fell immediately into place, and I was able to assemble a reasonable brief on his life to date. As a city dweller, I have always been amazed at the intimacy of village life, a cocoon which crumbles for the total stranger as soon as anyone reveals his family ties.

"Pitseolak!" I exclaimed, rising to shake his hand again. "Yes, of course! I've heard so much about you from Mangitak. How come we've never met before?"

He nodded in appreciation of my enthusiastic recognition, but before he could answer I was continuing, "When did you get back? Yesterday? There wasn't a plane today, was there?"

"No, not today. Actually, I got here last night. My mother came back on the same plane. She's been in Frobisher for hospital treatment. To be honest, we didn't expect to ever leave Frobisher because of the weather."

"How long have you been away?"

"Oh, just a few weeks. I left in early January." He spoke with the casualness of an experienced traveller. "I wasn't expecting my mother to fly in as well, on the same flight. They say that she is better now."

"Didn't you write and tell your father that you were due?"

"No. That's not the way we are," he replied rather ethnically, though artificially I thought. "When we go, we are not here, and when we return, we are. Eskimos are strange in a way. We accept everything and little surprises us."

"Are you pleased to be back?" I asked the question lamely, side-stepping the complex conundrum of his philosophy.

He shrugged his shoulders and, after a brief pause, replied, "Well, yes. I suppose so." Then he grinned and took a deep breath. "You see, I have to be where my family is, and to be truthful, when I am not with them, then I guess I feel a little homesick. Of course, now that I'm back and have seen everyone again — well, I wish I was going away again somewhere else. You know, this place is so small, and there really isn't much to do — other than sitting around the house and going out to visit people."

Suddenly he looked absurdly dejected, reminding me of a country boy who had got all dressed up to go to the local dance, only to find that it had been cancelled.

"Never mind," I said cheerfully. "You'll find plenty to do. After all, you've only just this minute got back here. How about a cup of coffee?"

"I'd love one, please. Haven't had a cup of decent coffee since I was in a discotheque in Montreal." He paused reflectively and added, "Like ages ago now."

As I stood up, he leant over the table and picked up the newspaper. From the kitchen, I could tell by the silence that he was already engrossed in it.

"It's a bit old!" I called out.

"Is it?" I could hear the pages rustling as he turned to find the date.

"Eight years old," I shouted. "Found it in the Hudson's Bay warehouse last week. Actually, I'd read well over half of it before it began to dawn on me that something was a bit strange. There's an article in there about Nasser going off to meet with King Hussein! Ay-ay, I said to myself — that's rather odd."

I heard him laugh and then go quiet again. It was then that it dawned on me that I had been forgetting he was a young Eskimo. I'd been chatting away at rapid speed without any conscious effort to think of vocabulary, and he hadn't had cause to ask me to stop or repeat anything. By habit, I usually modified my speech to make sure I was understood. Not so with Pitseolak. His entire disposition, attitudes, and mannerisms seemed so much like my own that I'd even presumed him to be familiar with developments in world politics.

"Nasser is dead, of course," I called out as an afterthought.

"Yes, I know. Sad."

During the next hour, we drank a lot of coffee, smoked, and superficially analysed the Middle East. Pitseolak was an avid listener, and he never hesitated to ask me to explain something that had gone beyond his own understanding. Above all, he seemed desperate to know — to learn about all things — and he was thus an ideal audience for someone like me who was only too willing to be able to indulge in such a conversation in this isolated corner of Baffin Island.

But even though we both enjoyed the passing of time, every so often I felt myself pausing for just a fragment of a second. This man was not really Eskimo. He didn't dress like one, nor indeed did he declare himself to have much in common with the Inuit. Here he was, his first night back home after being away for some time, and he was out visiting a complete stranger. I wondered what his family might think. But then it occurred to me that perhaps, in this, he was being typically Eskimo. As he had said earlier, "We don't always show much reaction or emotion. Nothing really surprises us. If you're here, you're here; if you're not, you're not." So I settled back and accepted that his family knew he was home and that there was no real point in extending the jubilation over several days.

"Well, I must go," he suddenly said, as if he had some other pressing engagement to keep. "Could I borrow this newspaper?"

"Sure! Please keep it. I've read it over and over again until I probably know every advert and every article. I even know that the editor's name is Arnold Devlin! Anyway, have it, and I'll let you know if I find any more, and you can have them after me."

"Thanks a lot. There's nothing to read in my parents' home. I really do like reading."

He threaded his boots, slipped his parka over his head, and was on his way with a cheery wave.

"Thanks for talking with me. I'll be back again, if you don't mind," he shouted over a shoulder.

"You're welcome any time," I replied, quickly slamming the door before too much snow blew inside.

I heard him crunch his way across the frozen snow, each footstep sounding like gentle tapping on a sheet of styrofoam. It was bitterly cold outside and the stars had been shining all day.

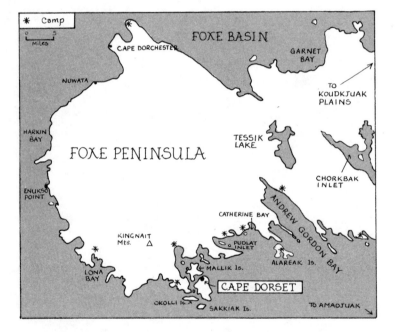

✳	Comp

0   5
Miles

FOXE BASIN

CAPE DORCHESTER

GARNET
BAY

NUWATA

TO
KOUDKJUAK
PLAINS

HARKIN
BAY

TESSIK
LAKE

FOXE PENINSULA

CHORKBAK
INLET

ENUKSO
POINT

CATHERINE BAY

ANDREW GORDON BAY

KINGNAIT
Mts. △

PUDLAT
INLET

ALAREAK Is.

LONA
BAY

MALLIK Is.

CAPE DORSET

OKOLLI Is.

SAKKIAK Is.

TO AMADJUAK

THE FOXE PENINSULA - BAFFIN ISLAND

TWO

As far as I was ever able to establish, Pitseolak had been born in 1945 somewhere near Lona Bay, along the southern edge of the Foxe Peninsula. Certainly, that is where he wished to have been born, as he told me on a couple of occasions. His eldest brother, Mangitak, seemed to have vague but distinct recollections of Pitseolak being there as a young boy, shortly before the family finally moved into that nucleus of dwellings that has grown into Cape Dorset.

He was the son of Oshoochiak and Etushakjuak, the second oldest surviving male of a union that eventually produced six children. Oshoochiak was a very kindly man with a round, pleasing face, the sort which naturally exudes cordiality, understanding, and sympathy. Born in 1908, Oshoochiak, like others of his age group, was an Eskimo from the traditional mould, raised to track and hunt in a region where survival was totally dependent on time-proven skills and inexhaustible initiative. He was a man of the land, a competent hunter, equipped by example since birth with all of the vital abilities that successful life demands of those who live in these arctic wastes.

Lona Bay is a desolate place, the rugged coastline gnawed and misshapen by the unrelenting pressure of sea ice for most of the year. Then, during the brief respite of summer, it is jolted by drifting icebergs and smashed by tireless waves. The rocks tumble and crack, breaking into sharp stones, which in turn disintegrate into a coarse greyish brown sand. Inland, barely beyond the immediate horizon, the scenery is monotonously beautiful, a continuing canopy of randomly scattered boulders — the debris of an ice age that has not yet stopped.

A narrow beach, invisible for much of the year, extends inwards slightly, flanked on either side by two jagged slopes; it allows a small tongue of frozen sea water to encroach a little onto the land. Walrus bounce their bellies across its gritty surface and become easy prey to the watchful hunter. To the north and inland, isolated herds of caribou prance with heads erect — statues at the scent of danger and graceful trotters when undisturbed. They too stumble in death at the whim of the hungry Eskimos.

Oshoochiak's tiny encampment used to merge perfectly into the setting — a large sealskin tent banked with warming snow so that it became invisible at a distance. From time to time, forever at the mercy of the seasonal habits of the animals on whom they relied for food, the family would move to other sites spread across what was viewed as their own natural territory — sometimes travelling for days or weeks until enough had been collected to satisfy empty stomachs. Then, with the sudden advent of spring, birds would speckle the vacant skies — arctic terns and geese migrating towards the Plains of Koudkjuak in order to breed and rear their young. But these, too, would become automatic targets for the hungry people below, affording a temporary change in diet and another means of surviving.

At the turn of the century, there were several family groups roaming the extremities of the Foxe Peninsula. They knew each other well, indeed, were often related, but their paths only crossed infrequently, as when they were in pursuit of the same stray caribou or when their migratory routes touched casually during a particular season. Other than this limited social contact, families grew and developed within themselves as inviolable units. Each child depended on the next for companionship, and all were reliant upon the knowledge of their parents for survival. Their days were spent hunting and playing, talking and listening to one another. Mother always had things to make and clothes to sew; father had constantly to ensure that the next meal was available when needed. It was an open life and free, although the environment imposed stringent boundaries on who went where, and when. The children knew never to wander and to be forever watchful for wolves and polar bear.

Sometimes, Pitseolak's brother Mangitak would go off with his father in search of food, using such opportunities to learn the habits and peculiarities of the prey; he would watch the moves of his skilful father, noticing when and how to make the fatal strike. They would track in the snow, or take a kayak out to the floe edge chasing seal.

"I remember," Mangitak told me, "that my mother used to get up very early each morning and make us tea or something hot to drink. Sometimes it was just water, or a soup made from fat. With her kudlik, it would take her an hour or even more just to heat up enough warm water for us to drink. The kudlik has seal oil in it, with lichens that burned like a wick. The kettle dangled above it, and we waited."

Being younger, Pitseolak usually stayed at home with the others, playing games and watching his mother prepare the meat with her curiously curved ulu — cutting fat from the skin of ujuk the seal and slicing the pelt into a long sinuous coil of strapping. Mangitak's experiences in the tundra were thus different from those of his younger brother. For just when Pitseolak was reaching that age when he too would be allowed to join them out hunting, the family began its tiring and final trek into Cape Dorset.

It was to prove itself more than just another move, more than just another place and another home. Without perhaps appreciating the true significance of the journey, Oshoochiak was taking his family from one culture to another. As they made their tracks across the snow and ice, the dogs pulling the long sled and the children often trotting alongside so as to keep warm, they were turning themselves away from the familiar, time-honoured way of life and moving into the arms of another. They could never be quite the same again; small subtle changes would overtake them all, often without their being aware of it. Some would adjust. But the small boy, sitting huddled close to his mother and wrapped in a bundle of caribou fur, would not.

The little party progressed gradually towards their new life, pausing for food and drink, stopping to hunt and to sleep. It was cold, and the young ones rubbed their faces and hands to avoid the telltale patches of white — the signs of frostbite. After many days, they paused at the base of Kingnait Mountain and looked across the rocky slopes that flowed from its curved summit. There they could clearly see the wooden, green-bordered compound of the Hudson's Bay trading post. The family of Oshoochiak had arrived.

It is impossible to know, now, how they felt at that moment; maybe just weary and tired. Nor can one tell how they viewed the future at that precise moment. In all probability they didn't give it a thought, for the uncertainty of living in the tundra has bred a philosophy centred on the present. For too many Inuit, tomorrow never comes. Certainly, as the travellers stood under the shadow of Kingnait that first day, they could not have guessed that twenty years later Oshoochiak would be aging gracefully as a church elder, that one brother would have become a famous carver, another an interpreter; that their mother would die in middle age and that Pitseolak would become the ill-fated heir of Nanook.

As the Hudson's Bay Company took an increasing interest in the potential of Baffin Island, the nomadic families proved to be more and more useful to the developers of this commercial empire. Like others, Oshoochiak entered their employ casually as a hunter, carrier, and guide, but later on he decided to join them permanently, and he moved his entire family into the cluster of houses which then encircled the Bay's store on Cape Dorset Island.

Cape Dorset settlement at that time must have been a strange and desolate outpost, consisting of half a dozen buildings perched on the northern shoreline facing adjacent Mallik Island. To and from the settlement would travel hunters with pelts to sell and ammunition to buy. They would camp themselves close by, dog teams tethered to stakes fastened into the ice, and there they would enjoy the conversation and friendship of other visiting families. Then, after a while, they would go back once more into the bleakness and silence of the barren land.

Alongside the family of Oshoochiak lived Peter Pitseolak, who was later to gain such great fame as an artist and photographer. "It was not like the community of today," he once told me. "There were few of us living here. Oshoochiak and his clan and just a couple of others. We all worked for the Hudson's Bay Company. We helped to collect their supplies from other depots, carrying them across the ice for many days and weeks at a time. It was hard work, but we liked it. The managers and their young clerks seemed to like being here too, and we always spent a lot of time together. We sang and told stories. We taught them about our ways, and they told us about theirs. One of the clerks, he came from Scotland, told me much about photography, and we spent many hours taking pictures and printing them onto special paper. But it was quiet, and often we didn't see anyone else for many weeks at a time."

Even this isolated community must have been a drastic

change for Oshoochiak and his family when they first arrived from Lona Bay, for they were exchanging the nomadic life for the sedentary, coming in from the open but precarious existence that they had always accepted and entering something that afforded different comforts and routines, but also security.

From the 1950s and through to the Diefenbaker years, the Canadian government began to implement a policy of encouraging the nomadic Inuit to live in settlements, and a great deal of money was spent creating larger communities around the existing trading centres. There were two main reasons for the policy. One was concern for the Inuit themselves, an awareness that as Canadian citizens they were entitled to the same rights and privileges as their countrymen farther south. Health and welfare programmes, education, and other services could be provided for them if they would agree to live in settled communities rather than wandering across the tundra in scattered family groups. Then there were the government's own administrative concerns: obviously it was far easier to handle a complete settlement than to try and keep track of unreachable families who might be anywhere within hundreds of miles. So the settlement policy was rigorously pursued.

With the passage of time, Oshoochiak learned the intricacies of filing income tax forms. The children reluctantly abided by routines that required them to be up at a specified time in the morning — rather than sleeping and waking whenever the need arose, as at camp. Pitseolak was enrolled at the local day school and began to learn new things. He proved to be an eager student, constantly curious, and he soon displayed a remarkable aptitude for English. The first in his family to attain any level of fluency in this weird foreign tongue, he especially enjoyed being able to talk with his teachers and with the construction workers and administrators in a language that the rest of his kinsfolk could not understand. He personified change and progress. He was the new generation.

Recognizing the boy's cleverness, his father eagerly consented when Pitseolak had the chance to be sent to Fort Churchill for further schooling. So Pitseolak went "south." And now, five years and some supplementary courses later — his English fluent — he was back in Cape Dorset, home for good.

And we had just been talking in my house for the first time.

Three

Cape Dorset is on the Foxe Peninsula of Baffin Island. When I was there, about five hundred people lived in the settlement, huddled in houses that clustered along the shoreline. Their home was on a small island some two hundred square miles in area, one of many such islands that speckle this southern coast. Trees have not been a feature of the landscape for many millions of years, and only the hardiest of grasses managed to break their way through the frozen soils. The countryside was bleak and barren, covered with snow for ten months of the year. Caribou roamed to the north and birds made their brief appearance during the spring and summer. Occasionally, wolves and polar bears ventured into the settlement, but on the whole the people lived a life that was undisturbed and slow-paced.

The houses were wooden; most were brought in by the government during the sixties. Before that, the Eskimos lived in tents and shacks made from whatever was available after the ships had made their annual visits. Cape Dorset was hardly a town, or even a village, although there was a community hall and several other buildings which comprised the Federal Day School. There was also a Hudson's

Bay Store and the locally owned co-operative; on the side of one hill, we even had an impressive-sounding "Go-go" club, large enough to contain one pool table, though it became crowded whenever more than twenty customers chose to congregate at the same time. The club faced southwards, looking out across the frozen sea towards a distant body of water called the Hudson Strait.

Three hundred miles west of Frobisher Bay and six hundred miles north of the nearest tree, the settlement could generously be classified as "isolated." But, for all of this, it was fascinating, a place of activity where people lived their lives with purpose.

I opened the curtains onto a beautiful Arctic morning. The blizzard was over. We were still in the dark period, with only a brief spell of twilight occurring just after noon, so the moon was high into a sparkling sky. It hovered just beyond Mallik Island, casting ripples of light across the adjacent sea ice. Without trees, and the snow frozen into rigid immobility, compacted by the wind, it was always difficult to assess the true nature of the day's weather. I put my ear to the chimney and, hearing no sounds, presumed that all was calm outside. The thermometer read -28°F.

As an Arctic news correspondent for CBC at Frobisher Bay, and also in my role of community teacher, I prided myself on having seen, met, or spoken with the majority of the people in the settlement. But, somehow or the other, Pitseolak didn't seem to have featured before, and this had been nagging at me ever since he had left the previous evening.

"I feel I have met him somewhere before," I said, primarily to myself. "I know that I have. Just can't place him."

"Well, I don't know him," commented my wife. "At least, from your description, he could be any one of a dozen or so people. I'm sure I would have remembered his style of dress, if nothing more." Since Jill had been out, acting as Tawney Owl for the local Brownie troop the previous evening, she wasn't as obsessed by Pitseolak as I was.

"I wonder what it was that prompted him to come in for a visit in the first place," I said.

"Heaven knows!" Jill exclaimed. Then, casually, she added, "Perhaps because he was bored and had already visited everyone else for miles around."

We finished breakfast and then, as I was feeding my feet gently into my kamiks, it came to me. "It was Christmas! About twelve-thirty on Christmas morning — down there on the ice. That's it! I knew I'd seen him before!"

I felt relieved. My reputation for never forgetting a face was still intact. And I could see it all quite clearly now. During the brief spell of daylight on Christmas Day, we had left the house and ambled down the slope, past the other houses, past the Bay, and onto the sea ice. Someone had organized a series of games for the people of the community, and there were little groups scattered all over the place — watching, participating, chatting. It was a scene of collective activity, a happening that appeared to involve us all to some extent or other.

Up on the flat area in front of the store, some of the men were having a shooting contest. They were squatting in that familiar Eskimo stance, one leg curled under the body to provide a seat, as they took aim at a block of wood mounted well below and far away in the middle of the whiteness.

"Have a go," someone urged. So I copied everything I had seen the others doing — position and poise. However, the target was so far off that I had to ask where it was; and my volley of three shots was so badly directed that no one even saw the bursts of snow shoot up from beyond the stake. But, then, I had never been one to win a fluffy dog at the fairgrounds, and none of the hunters watching me expected this particular kadloona to be a threat to their prized marksmanship. Later, out of curiosity, I made my way to see precisely what it was that I had been aiming at and found half an ace of hearts tacked to a small board — the heart shape long since obliterated by bullet holes.

Mangitak joined me at the shooting range, and we walked together across the sled tracks, through the broken, fractured tidal ice, and across to the field events. And that was when I first saw Pitseolak. He was standing in a line with thirty or so other men, wearing a yellow skidoo suit and breathing into his cupped hands. Then he rubbed them together — just as he had last night.

As I recalled the scene, I realized that it was he who had beckoned me to join the running race. Standing beside me, he had explained the route. "Right over there to the oil drums and then curve around that way until you get back to this line," he had said, one foot pointing at a mark that an elderly man was raking into the snow with the butt of a rifle.

Then...off! We all started the race in a line, though it soon became ragged and uneven as we charged as competitors, and slipped and fell on the rough surface. We gained the oil drums and began to charge back. It was at this point that most of us plunged into a deceptive snowbank. We were well up to the armpits before we realized what had happened. It was so cold that I was one of the first out. Turning, I saw that Pitseolak was still churning in the mass of snow, laughing and flapping his arms, a figure sinking into a bed of foam.

"Yes! That's when I first saw Pitseolak," I told Jill triumphantly. "On Christmas Day. I knew we'd met before!"

Relieved that I had now satisfied my memory, I walked out into the morning freshness and towards Mangitak's house. Mangitak lived next door, and we had developed one of those rare friendships during a short time, the type of relationship in which you are soon close friends, or brothers even; uncannily, we seemed to have been together since childhood. With my very limited Eskimo and his equally sparse knowledge of English, we had developed the art of communication to its fullest, and hours were spent laughing, telling jokes, and discussing a fine array of topics.

Pitseolak's brother Mangitak was a carver of stature who had already had work displayed at major galleries in several Canadian cities. But he was also a hunter, the brother born ahead of Pitseolak in time and therefore raised into the culture of the tundra. It was he who had learned to track and understand the signs that would mean health or starvation. So, whenever the need arose, he would leave his artist's tools, take up a rifle, and seek the seals at the floe edge or find caribou in the desolate spaciousness of the encircling wastes. He had a delightful family of four girls, and he and his wife were forever in our home.

Passing his house that morning, in keeping with a standard agreement, I banged on all of the glass windows and kicked the outer walls with gusto.

"Wakey, wakey!" I shouted without stopping.

Mangitak had recently acquired a permanent job in the local print shop, peeling off limited editions of highly prized works of art from the hand-carved master stone. At his request, therefore, I was to sound this boisterous reveille — presuming that if he slept through the din then at least the odds were in favour of one of the other members of the family waking up.

His sister Martha was one of the students at the school. She was short, with black flowing hair and long, dark eyelashes. Coupled with her brownish complexion and infectious smile, it was more than apparent that she was developing into a most attractive young lady. And when she ruffled her hair into deliberately antagonizing untidiness, or glared with her dark eyes, there was enough wildness about her to have made her a photographer's dream elsewhere.

She spoke good English, when she wanted to, but like other moody adolescents she frequently chose to do nothing of the sort — chattering in Eskimo, with unpleasant undertones and a meanly pouted lip; but she would generally end the barrage with a warm infectious laugh.

"Pitseolak came visiting last night," I remarked casually as she entered school that day.

"Yes, I know!" It was a pleasant response, but she said no more, and I was left wondering what he had said and what extra bits of information she now knew about me.

Schooldays consisted essentially of a sequence of "southern" routines peppered with spells of reading, writing, and talking in English — the latter being the all-embracing and ultimate object of everything that was done. Perhaps it was not very inspiring. On the other hand, it was a contrast to the students' daily life and therefore retained maybe a novelty factor, which in turn sustained most of the children for the prescribed amount of time each day. But it was different. There was a set time established when the morning bell would ring — curious in a culture where people slept when and where they happened to feel tired and woke when they were no longer tired. During the day, other bells would ring to indicate a change of subject, which was another oddity to children used to keeping at something interesting until they lost interest. Cocoa was served at a precise time each morning, when the bell once more uttered its clang — and some found it strange that we all had to drink because the bell said so, rather than because we were thirsty. Then it would ring again and we were allowed to go home.

"You kadloonas do what a bell tells you," one young boy had remarked, mildly angered because the ringing had indicated that lessons began again. "I'm still thirsty! I haven't finished my drink!" He shook his head in total disbelief, muttering, "*We* do what our bodies tell us to do, not some noisy old bell!"

This introduction of formal and rigid routines was clearly necessary if anyone was to receive an education in the government-run school system, but it was in stark opposition to the people's own way of life in which opportunity, circumstances, and desire dictated their actions.

Released by the bell, I wandered off to get some canned milk from the Hudson's Bay store — and Pitseolak and I physically collided by the corner of the house. After apologies, we turned in the same direction and went off to do my shopping.

"What do you send in those news reports of yours?" Pitseolak asked. "I mean, what is there to say about this little place where nothing happens from one day to the next?"

With a smile, I explained. "Well, in the first place, there's always something going on everywhere, anywhere. It may be important, maybe not — but there is always going to be something happening."

"Not here," he murmured sullenly.

"Okay," I began, determined not to lose him before I had even begun to answer his question. "Let's take a man locked in a small, dark cell. It's empty. Nothing in it. No carpet, chair, sink, nothing." Pitseolak had his head lowered, but I knew that he was imagining what I had suggested. "Well, that man sits there day in, day out, day in...for days, weeks, and years. Now, I'll wager you that within a very short period of time he will have begun to notice all manner of things in that room that he hadn't seen at first. Things like cracks — the patterns they make; the shapes of damp spots; the tiles on the floor; or the floorboards with their streaked, knotted surfaces. In short, he will eventually be able to keep himself totally absorbed in this confined world of his, always seeing new things." I glanced at Pitseolak. He was watching his rubber boots step over the tracks that others had made beneath our feet. "See what I'm getting at?" I enquired.

"Yep, I see what you're saying. But I still want to know what sort of things you find to include in a regular radio programme, when all you report on is this dead-end place!"

"All right, let's see!" We climbed to the top of the shop stairs and paused outside, leaning on a green, peeling railing in front of the store. I took off my mittens and held the tips of my fingers as I began to give him specific areas that were normally included in my newscast.

"Things of general interest. I guess it's a sort of weekly account of what happens here — rather like a contemporary history if you like. There are things like births and deaths. Hunting — who is out, where they are, what they catch, how much they get. Then the weather, temperatures, snow depths, position of the ice edge, thickness of the ice in the region of the landing strip. All manner of things like this, plus anything else that might crop up. A polar bear around the edge of the community some months back was a neat story to do something on, for example."

Pitseolak nodded, partially satisfied. "But why should anyone be at all interested in these things? I mean, who cares that Pingwartok caught three caribou last week and nearly lost a finger from frostbite because it was so cold? I mean, who really cares?" He shook his head, then stood combing his hair back into shape again.

"Well," I said, "first of all, there are folk who are genuinely curious to know precisely the sort of things that do go on up here. Then there are maybe people in other settlements who, like Frobisher, can pick up these transmissions and who might even find companionship within their own isolation simply by hearing what someone else is doing." I paused, thought, and proceeded. "Then there might be relatives who want to hear what is happening in their own community while they are away — your mother in hospital in Frobisher Bay for example. And possibly others listen because they are fascinated by titbits and hope for a gem they can gossip about, or some obscure fact they can parade around the cocktail circuit!" I laughed at my own last comment.

"It wouldn't interest me!" He dismissed my explanation with a shrug. "I'd like to know more about what is going on in the South. I'd like to hear some music and international news — not a whole load of meaningless stuff about some tinpot little place like this up here in the heart of nowhere!"

His attitude worried me, not so much because it might put me into the queues of the unemployed, but because it was narrow minded and intolerant. I didn't believe he was being honest.

"Not even if there was the prospect of hearing news about your own family?" I challenged, leaning on my elbows but looking straight at him.

He hesitated — a slight concession to possibility. Then he said, "Maybe, but then if it was that important, they'd let me know about it anyhow."

"But, as an Eskimo, wouldn't you be vaguely interested in listening to something that was about your homeland? About what is being hunted at a particular time of the year — albeit just to check that it's normal? Wouldn't you be slightly curious to know where the caribou were — maybe that they'd moved since last you went hunting? I mean, wouldn't you at least react with some level of interest if you heard that millions of walrus had overrun your home town? Or that the snow had stopped falling on Baffin Island? Or that all of the ice had melted up here, for ever?

Or that an epidemic had wiped out every living Eskimo?"

I knew that the illustrations were becoming bizarre, but I was disconcerted by his total disinterest in all things about his homeland.

He was laughing at some of the prospects I had presented.

"Of course I'd be interested." He went silent, but then added, "But many of the things wouldn't interest me at all!"

We went inside. I bought the milk, asked how long it had been in the store, and the assistant replied, "Since Nansen." It was a joke, but one always felt it to be possible.

"Do you know, Pitseolak," I said as we left through the door, "that I sat having a plate of cornflakes for breakfast last month. I also sat doing the puzzle and competition on the back of the box. When I finished it, I read the directions and rules for entry — just because I had already read every other word that was printed on it — and the closing date for the competition was not only three months gone but was two years earlier!"

We were still laughing as we rounded the shop's large deep-freeze unit and started making our way up the slope leading to both our houses.

"Are you really as disinterested in this whole place as you make out?" I asked as we padded cautiously along.

He thought, sifted his reaction, and then chose to be honest: "Yes, I really am. They know what they're doing. They've chosen it all. I've simply chosen to do other things, see other places. I don't want to be hemmed in here all my life — sitting in a wooden house looking at the snow. I want to be somewhere else, learning other things. Meeting other people. We all have our choices to make and I've made mine. You see, ever since I went to school and started to learn so many different things, I've kind of drifted away from the values and attitudes of my father, my family, and many of my friends. The things that satisfy them can no longer satisfy me. It's as simple as that. I'm from another generation I suppose." He shrugged his shoulders and raised upturned hands. "This igloo bit just isn't my bag, as we say!" He grinned.

We had reached the steps outside my house — actually, there were six of these steps, long wooden planks encased in metal frames, but each had been systematically buried by snowfalls over the preceding six months. Where we were standing, it should have been in the vicinity of step number five.

"But it's difficult for me," I said, "to appreciate that you could have turned your back on it all so completely. I'm English for example, although I haven't lived there permanently for ages. But whenever I see the coastline of the country, either from the air or sea, then I do react. I still have a strong identity with that country — because it's where I was born. I'll always be a part of it, or it will always be a part of me. I just don't think that any of us can turn off quite as tightly as you say you have."

"But it is different for me," he pleaded, trying to convince me. "I couldn't build an igloo to save my life. I really wouldn't be certain how to go about it. I know that they use a special type of snow, packed and frozen in a certain way — but I just wouldn't know which type it was. Anyway, if it came to it, I'd prefer a tent. But, then, is there any reason for me to be ashamed of that? I mean, could you build one of the things if you had to?"

"I'd probably have a go and make an absolute ass of myself," I admitted.

"Same here!" It was that simple. "And I'd take a neat little fold-up cooker with a gas bottle, a sleeping bag, and, knowing myself as I do, I'd also want a rubber blow-up bed to lie on."

"The modern Eskimo!" I jested, hand held high on his

shoulder as if presenting him to a large but invisible audience. "Ladies and gentlemen, step right up and meet the Modern Eskimo — Pitseolak!"

He bowed to the barren hillside, clasped his hands high above his head like some prize fighter and said "Thank you." He also caught the reflection of my quizzical wife in the window and scampered off, waving: "She'll think I'm mad or something!"

But as I removed several layers of clothing in the outer hallway, I couldn't help thinking that his attitudes were somehow naive; they were scarcely real. I began to wonder just how much they were a front, the easy way out, an explanation partly for himself to say, "I don't want to be here. I don't fit in here." He claimed to have shed his own people and background all too easily and thoroughly. I just didn't think it possible. It was unnatural to be so remote from one's roots. Surely, nobody could ever succeed in shaking loose from those? Footballers and soldier heroes return to their villages in triumph; self-made millionaires return to view their humble origins; old people return to their homelands for a last look. All of this is fundamental to basic human nature, to curiosity or vanity.

It was clear that Pitseolak's manner of self-confidence had been nurtured among the flashing lights of coffee houses and discotheques, and had flourished in a fantasy world of trendy clothes and droves of adoring girls. But these things just did not exist here; they didn't count. Personal value was assessed by an individual's true personality and social worth. Nobody played games up here; you had to be honest with yourself in order to survive.

I wondered how long it would be before he stepped beyond the artificial lighting of his deliberately perpetuated dream. He was back but could not accept it. I realized that sooner or later he would have to lower his guard and face reality. Nobody can shadow-box for ever.

Four

A few weeks later Pitseolak's mother was dead. Actually, Kanikpellik was his stepmother, having married Oshoochiak in 1964. With this union, the family subsequently swelled to approximately ten — a mixture of brothers, sisters, half brothers, adopted brothers, and stepbrothers.

She had returned from Frobisher Bay on Tuesday, 21 January, following treatment for a miscellany of ailments. Although not a well woman, sadly riddled with tuberculosis and severely underweight, no one expected that scarcely three weeks later she would be dead.

That fatal night is as clear in my mind as it was clear in the sky. A bitterly cold night, with a contrastingly soft breeze picking up the snow and coaxing it to land a few feet farther on. Under the lights, large fluffy flakes of whiteness fluttered around the lamps like a myriad of carefree moths. I was out walking, going nowhere, just deciding whom to visit.

It was one of those peculiar occasions when hindsight suggests that some sort of greater power may have intervened and redirected my course. It had happened to me once before when, as a child, I had approached the door of a friend's house and then decided to go away; I later learned his father was dying at that precise moment. I glanced at my watch. It was 7.20 and I walked past Oshoochiak's home. At 7.25 Kanikpellik was dead.

The house had been full of people for well over an hour. Children running around freely, shouting, pushing, pulling, chasing, being noisy; the men standing along the walls talking loudly and peering casually over the shoulders of a cluster of women who squatted on the floor, playing cards. I had never fully understood the game, possibly some type of poker that had been modified by local rules to such an extent that it was, at that point, beyond recognition. But it involved a great deal of laughter, slapping cards on the deck, taking others, calling out and depositing five-cent bets.

At the height of the boisterous revelry, Kanikpellik suddenly lurched forward and collapsed in a bundle amidst the scattering of cards and coins. Instant silence preceded instant pandemonium as people screamed, were restrained, and cried again. Mangitak and Pitseolak gently keeled the rigid figure onto its side and then rolled it onto the floor. Alternately, they tried mouth-to-mouth resuscitation, whilst Oshoochiak called the Mission House. But it was all to no avail. She was dead.

From the bottom of the hill, I glanced across the snow-banks and noticed Mike, the missionary, racing up the slope. Without further thought, I ambled on my aimless way, unaware of the screeching, crying, and yelling that had just exploded within the house at the top of the incline.

It was morning before Jill and I became aware of the family's tragedy, and by then there were no signs of grief. Just a strange sense of acceptance, the reaction that Eskimos so often display in the wake of disaster. Martha calmly told me she would be absent from school that afternoon so that she could attend her mother's funeral. Mangitak sauntered casually into the house at noon and invited us to the funeral. Gone were the tear-stained eyes and fretful faces. Death is a finality that the People accept, realizing that lengthy grief and overt sorrow can never undo its unpleasant work. A mother was dead. As Pitseolak had said to me, "When we're gone, we're gone."

In the remoteness of the tundra, funerals are stripped of the soothing and comforting pretensions to which most of us are accustomed: there can be no cortege and no solemn procession of cars along pathways of neat, white head-stones. There are no tenderly trimmed lawns to guide the way; no swaying trees overhead to sprinkle autumnal leaves over the bare heads of the mourners. There is nothing.

After a brief service in the small church, the body of Kanikpellik was carried out into the fierce blizzard. The plywood box, assembled from some spare packing-case wood, was crudely fashioned. Without handles or glasslike polished surface, screws pinioned the corners and nails gripped the jagged side joints. As it was borne over the rocks, feet slipped and slid on the ice and snow without control, and random helping hands pushed and pulled to prevent it from falling. On a slight rise, some large boulders had been rolled aside; no neatly cut grave, for digging in the permafrost is impossible. The box was placed in the centre of the clearing, not in the ground but on it, and the stones were hastily piled up until no wood was visible.

No one paused or lingered at the graveside, it was too cold and bitter, the temperature a long way below zero. Mike said a few words for the departed soul and we hur-riedly turned our backs on Kanikpellik and retreated from the freezing gusts of wind. I paused to glance back at that crude resting place and thought of the frail woman in the fragile box. But the recent scuffle-marks and fresh mound of stones were already obliterated by the endless blanket of sparkling white that extended from horizon to horizon. It was as if none of us had ever been there. Within just a few minutes, I couldn't even make out where the grave was, and in a day or so I would probably be unable to find it at all — unless the wolves visited. "When we're gone, we are gone."

Supper that evening was a sober and tasteless affair, indulged in more as a ritual than a necessity. It was simply time to eat, and we ate mechanically, without knowing or needing anything. Alone but together, Jill and I were both thinking of the concealed mound so recently abandoned somewhere back over there. It was somehow difficult to think of Kanikpellik now as a person. Rather, Pitseolak's mother had become a carcass left out to the elements in a wooden box. It was not even a cadaver wrapped in a shroud and covered with warm blankets. I could still vividly hear the rigid movements of her body, denied the comforts of plush padding and satin cushions, as it had bounced and jerked across the bare wood on the way to the grave. I had wondered then whether the shaking and knocking had bruised her white frozen skin. I wondered still.

Jill cleared the table. We had pecked at everything and eaten nothing.

"No cross! No flowers!" she muttered.

Somehow even the thought of a bunch of cottongrass placed on the spot in spring became pretentious and almost sacrilegious to the naked, primitive landscape. It was weird to encounter death up here in the icy wastes of the Arctic — no mention in the obituary columns, just a thin blue line drawn across another name in the government Eskimo Disk List, done with a pencil and ruler in the resident Mountie's house over a cup of steaming coffee. He'd report it over the radio-telephone as a matter of form, alongside the other incidental events of the week; and Kanikpellik would simply cease to exist. In years to come, her name might be forgotten too.

There were other graves that I had encountered on Cape Dorset Island, and three in particular always remained fixed in my mind. Jill and I had stumbled on them quite by accident one day when we had been out on a long exploratory walk, long before winter had confirmed its grip. Suddenly, there they were: two large piles of pebbles and a smaller one nearby, neatly framed by strips of wood that had since rotted into a silver-greyish colour. Only one of the fashioned crosses remained erect, and we had paused to restake the others. We guessed that this must be a family — father, mother and child — who had perished somehow, sometime, in the middle of nowhere. We couldn't even discern the name, other than that it ended in "sven." And there were neither records nor recollections of the family in Cape Dorset.

But, although largely ignored, there was one major grave in the settlement which was not neglected or forgotten: that of the legendary Pootoogook. He was undoubtedly the greatest of all the Eskimo camp leaders who lived on Baffin Island in this century — a powerful man, whose personality, build, and abilities automatically demanded respect; a leader whose territorial control is said to have spanned roughly half of the entire length of Baffin and whose final base for aid, advice, and loyalty was Cape Dorset. Neatly edged with a white picket fence, the grave of Pootoogook sits on a low-lying spur overlooking the community. While the other burial mounds scattered across the tundra could be — were — anybody, the uniqueness of perpetual presence had been bestowed on Pootoogook.

I could see his distant grave from my living-room window and was gazing at it thoughtfully that evening when suddenly my vision telescoped back to six feet just in time to catch sight of Pitseolak tapping the glass as he bounded up the steps into the house. I braced myself for those awkward few moments that inevitably arise when one has to convey condolences. This proved unnecessary.

"Hi!" said Pitseolak as he landed squarely in the centre

of the room. He was rubbing his hands to stimulate the sensations of his skin. "How is everyone this evening?"

"Sorry about your mother," I muttered. He curled his lips, raised his eyebrows, and jerked his head to one side. I had once seen someone show the same expression of resignation in front of a bookie's kiosk after losing a bet at the race track.

"Yes," Pitseolak replied calmly. "She was a good woman." The epitaph was over.

"What's your father doing?"

"Oh, he's having supper tonight with Mike over at the Mission House. I don't know what the rest of them are doing. Audla's at home listening to some records. Saila is getting ready to go hunting, I believe. I think he's going off again in the morning."

"What are you going to do with yourself?" I asked, thinking of our conversation at the Bay. "You can't just sit around doing nothing for ever, can you?"

"I really don't know."

"What do you do for money? I mean, you at least need it for clothes — and that after-shave lotion you use!"

He chuckled at the gentle dig. "I don't know," he repeated.

"Well, where do you get your money from?"

"From my father. He gives it to me when I ask."

"But you can't go on doing that ad infinitum, can you?"

"No, but what else can I do? There's no work around here for me to do, is there?"

"But I'm sure you could go and find work in Frobisher if you really wanted to. You know that yourself."

"What you must realize," he began, "is that for us Eskimos, the place where we have to be and want to be is where our families are. This is something that none of you seem to understand! For us, the family is very important. We do not like to be split up and parted." He glanced at me accusingly. "I do not see how you can be happy. Your

42

mother is in England, your sister in Vancouver — and you are up here. How can you honestly say that you are a close family when you all live so far apart? How can you always tell me that you are close when you don't even see each other for many months or years?"

I didn't attempt to explain this all over again. I had done so once before, and clearly he was unable to accept such a possibility. To him, close proximity, a touchable distance, was vital to keeping the family unit intact. Our cultures were too far apart.

During the slight pause that followed, I tried to think of some jobs that might be available for Pitseolak. It wasn't very easy, for work in the settlement was rather limited. There wasn't a great deal that he could do.

At last, I suggested: "You could always do some drawings and sell them to the print shop — you'd get about five dollars a time, and you'd make a fortune if you sat down for regular hours each day and did a set number of drawings."

"I can't draw," he said without hesitation.

"Now, come on! I've seen some of your drawings. You remember the ones you brought over one lunch hour, done in black lead pencil?" They had been very good, detailed and precise: stylized Eskimo figures set in delicately hachured backgrounds. One had shown a mountain goat — a memorized relic from his school days.

Pitseolak blushed. Despite his modesty, he knew that he could draw well.

"But you know as well as I that that's no way to make a living," he said. "It's false! Everyone around here does it — you don't have to be good. Anyone can scribble on a bit of paper and sell it to the Co-op. They buy virtually anything. All of us can't be that good that we can sell any old picture scratched on a bit of paper. Why pretend we're all artists when we're not?

"I can't do that," he repeated. "It would be sham,

artificial! I'm not an artist, and I know it. I wouldn't be able to make a living at it anywhere else in the world, except for here. The others don't understand this, they perhaps don't care. But I do!" Then, as if to ramify the point, he added, "In any case, all of this business of Eskimo art can't last for ever. Then what would I do?"

His argument was valid. The entire concept of Eskimo art embraced not only the true artists of the community — of which there were in fact many — but it also extended to all Eskimos, whether they could carve or not and whether they had any artistic sense whatsoever. Daily, I had seen chunks of stone hacked to pieces with gay abandon until some vague shape suggested itself. With a couple of circles scratched for eyes, it became a seal; another hack, and a bit dropped off — so it became a fish! I had long contended that the future of Eskimo art would have to rest with the publicizing of the genuine artists and their artwork, and that the work of the true artists should be separated from the rest. Pitseolak's brother Mangitak was one of the real artists — talented, capable and skilful. And obviously Pitseolak felt it would be pretentious to produce pictures or carvings side by side with Mangitak.

"All right," I conceded. "Well then....What about going down to the DNA office? The Department of Northern Affairs is always hiring people to help in the office. They might need someone to be a clerk — and your knowledge of English is excellent. You never know, they may want someone down there to deal with correspondence and help write reports. Can you type?"

"Just a little. With two fingers and a lot of mistakes."

"Well, you could always come up here and practise on my machine," I offered. "Learn to type and, with your English, you could probably be sent off on some courses by the government and get yourself trained for something with them. You could even take over a good permanent job right here, but you've got to be prepared to go out and help yourself. Nothing will come up to you, as you sit at home."

"I guess that I could go down and see what they've got going in the morning," he agreed. "But I know that they recently hired Panepak to do all the repainting, and that just before Christmas they didn't have anything for Ooviloo when she came back from Frobisher."

"But that's some time back. Try again. Sit down with the administrator and ask him what you could possibly do there. Ask him if there are any courses you could go on that would help you to qualify for a job back home. I've seen loads of circulars mentioning all manner of opportunities — and many of them are calling out for Eskimos to take over more and more different jobs. It's your time," I encouraged him. "I'd have thought that any keen young Eskimo who is as fluent in English as you are would be in great demand with the department. At least go and ask — talk to them and find out what's going on."

He sat there rubbing his chin, considering my suggestion.

"Okay," he said eventually, "if you think there's any point. But, you know, it seems to me that I have spent all of these years being taught how to learn English, and why? All I can use it for is to speak to the teachers who taught me. None of it — actually not any of the stuff the kadloonas taught me in their schools — is much use up here. My father can't speak English, and I obviously wouldn't need to speak in English to Martha. In a way, it's all a waste of time, isn't it. Why did they bother to teach me all these useless things?"

He spoke with emotion. Obviously this was a sore point.

"You know something?" he asked. I shrugged my shoulders. "I wonder why they bother to make us learn all these things. Why do they make us know about oak, elm, and maple trees, when there are none up here and never will be? Why do we have to know about the musk ox when they don't live this far south? We don't really care about those explorers who came into the land of the Eskimos — like Frobisher, Baffin, and Bylot." He stopped suddenly and took a sighing breath, as if to say that he wasn't accusing me personally. "Well, all I'm saying is that while I was learning all these things and going to Churchill, no one was teaching me the ways of my own people. And now I can't hunt and I know nothing about how to survive in the icy lands. You've messed me up!"

In a sense, he was right. He had learned our ways at the expense of his own, and he was the poorer for it. For there was no way any kadloona could survive up here without the time-proven skills of the Inuit. Rasmussen and Nansen had known that, and they had learned from the Eskimos before embarking on their exploits; it was the obvious thing to do in such a hostile land. Yet we, with all the advantages of contemporary science, seemed to be working in the opposite direction. It did seem rather odd, and it was difficult to explain the philosophy to Pitseolak. But the fact remained that we could not deny him or his people such things as schooling. The Inuit were entitled to the same opportunities as other Canadians.

As I sat there looking thoughtful, Pitseolak added: "Don't get me wrong, now. It's just that most of the things we learn at school are no use when we go and hunt and camp. If we were taught those things too, then perhaps people of my age wouldn't be so useless in our own land."

He had a good point there. Much of the education was inappropriate, though this wasn't always recognized. Some months earlier, long before Christmas, a pair of psychiatrists had come to the settlement to complete a series of tests on the Eskimo children, and when I had asked about the findings, one of them had replied, "At this stage, all I can say is that Eskimo youngsters are an average of two years retarded when compared to their counterparts in the South."

"They're what?" I asked, unashamedly aghast.

"Two years retarded."

"What sort of questions were on the papers?"

"Oh, the elementary sort of things, nothing special. Questions asking them to fit shapes into openings and to identify basic trees and so on."

"Trees?" I shot back. "How can they identify trees when there are none up here?"

"Oh, only simple ones — maple, larch, birch — you know, the ones that all children know from kindergarten."

It was very obvious that the test had not been regionalized, yet this didn't seem to have been taken into account when forming conclusions. When I raised the point, the psychiatrist explained that the trees in the testing programme were part of the children's realm of exposure through books and magazines. That none of them had seen or touched a single leaf was immaterial.

"Naturally," he concluded, "such tests should ideally be regionalized, but then this isn't a federally sponsored evaluation, so it's all right as it is."

I couldn't agree. An entire ethnic unit was being branded as retarded when, in so many ways, these children's resilience, initiative, and responsiveness were blatantly superior to many others of their age groups.

Thinking of Pitseolak's complaints, I realized that the whole thing was a circle, endless as a discussion. So I brought Pitseolak back to the simpler problem — his own immediate future — pressing him to go to the DNA office.

"Okay," he said, "in the morning. Or at least in the next day or so."

Knowing that I couldn't pin him down further, I left it at that.

Five

It was about a week later that I next saw Pitseolak, and he seemed excited as he came striding into the house. "Tell me about the wolves," he said.

"Wolves?" The wolf incident had happened a couple of months earlier. Had someone at the DNA office mentioned it? I had been wondering how Pitseolak's search for work had gone — and was still wondering — but was reluctant to press him in case he had been disappointed. This was perhaps a mistake. If I had known the truth, I would certainly not have sat comfortably in my chair satisfying his curiosity about the wolves.

"There isn't really much to tell," I said.

"But tell me anyway. I want to hear."

"Well," I began after a slight pause, "we'd been sitting over there by the window with Marianne — you know, the new teacher. She'd just arrived, as it happens, that same afternoon from Frobisher. The curtains were open wide so that she could look out over the settlement while we told her about the various houses and buildings that we can see from here."

"It was December, wasn't it?"

"Yes, end of December, or possibly the first day or so of January."

"You and my brother went after them, didn't you?" Pitseolak asked with unexpected eagerness.

"Yes, Jill and Marianne and I had been sitting and talking, as I said, when suddenly these two wolves passed in front of the window. Funnily enough, Marianne had been asking about wild animals and I'd just told her that we'd never seen anything in the settlement!"

Pitseolak smiled.

"Actually, at first, I thought that they were two stray huskies, but there was something about their tails and the urgency of their eyes and movements that suggested they weren't just regular dogs. They came from behind us," I said, arcing my arm to the far corner of the room and the emptiness that lay out the back.

I thought carefully and spoke slowly as the scene came back to me. "One was greyish in colour, perhaps with a few dashes of brown in its coat. The other, I seem to recall, was more white. Anyway, we watched them go by the steps and then disappear around the back of Paulassie's house." I pointed and Pitseolak followed.

"It was the first time that I'd ever seen wolves around the houses — in fact, they were the first live ones I'd ever seen in the wild. It was unreal! We all knew they were dangerous and doubly so to risk coming into the settlement looking for food. Only a few days before this, Mangitak had been telling us about a child who had been badly mauled by a wolf at one of the camps some time ago. I can't remember who it was, but I know that he said the child nearly died."

Pitseolak didn't offer a name, so I carried on: "After some minutes had passed and there'd been no further sign of movement, I dashed outside and across to Mangitak — his house being in the opposite direction, of course! Without waiting, he jumped up, grabbed his rifle, and ran out into the snow, asking me to show him exactly where I'd seen them. When I pointed out their path, he fell onto his knees, fingered the snow, and said, 'Amaro!' "

"Wolves," translated Pitseolak thoughtfully.

"We then followed the tracks for a few yards until Mangitak had satisfied himself that there were two animals. Then it seemed to dawn on him that they must have come close by his own house as well as mine. He stood for a few moments in silence. Then he patted me quietly on the shoulder and we went back for his skidoo."

I glanced at Pitseolak. He was listening carefully, with the same intensity and excitement that I was re-experiencing myself. I could feel the cold whipping against my ears and the bite on the tips of my fingers, could hear the snow crunch under our feet as we had started the motor and gently eased the skidoo out of the crusty ice.

"I was holding the rifle. Mangitak drove, slowly, glancing down at the tracks. I hadn't seen the first ones. They were nothing but distorted blemishes in the white. But by Paulassie's house they became clearer. We stopped and listened. Nothing. Mangitak got off the skidoo and hurried on along for a short way, bending, looking down. Then he ran back and, without saying anything, we went farther towards your father's house. It was such a beautiful, clear night. A night without sounds, other than the sober whistling of the wind. It was odd, in a way, that in the midst of all of this, we two were trying to find a couple of dangerous animals — while no one else seemed to know that they were around. I know they actually stopped right outside your house. In fact, they went underneath and stole some meat that your father had been storing!"

Pitseolak lost all expression and stared blankly.

"We followed the tracks right up to your back door. Mangitak got off the skidoo again and crawled on his hands and knees looking under the house. There were some very clear scuffle-marks by the wire netting — even I could see what had happened! Then, we went on farther, the footprints becoming clearer and clearer. By Ootoochie's house and then over the bank at the back. We were now going along with the wolves, but still hadn't spotted them. They had taken their food and were heading back to their young. At one point, the snow had become very deep and one of the wolves had obviously slipped down quite deeply before it could get out. There were signs that the other had stopped and walked around it in a small circle."

I had seen the whole scene most vividly at the time, the wolf's hind legs perhaps buried in the snowdrift, while its mate walked around anxiously, eyes on the lookout, ready to pounce on anything that moved nearby.

Pitseolak stirred slightly in the chair and I carried on talking.

"I know that I began to feel that they were very close. We were both now actually looking for them. Their tracks were spread out clearly ahead and we expected them to appear any second. We went down the slope that leads to Etungak's house, saw the disturbed snow, and made a detour away from it and down towards the sea ice. At the bottom of a small valley, Mangitak stopped the skidoo, left me with the rifle, and clambered up a slight rise on his own. Sitting alone, clutching the rifle, I suddenly realized that I wasn't even sure how to fire the thing, let alone aim it at an advancing wolf which might be about to attack the pair of us!"

I could feel the goose pimples rising on my arms, just as they had that night out there in the snow.

"It was very quiet," I continued, "and I strained for the slightest sound of anything. I couldn't even hear Mangitak. Nothing. No sound of anything. Then it dawned on me that Mangitak might have scared the wolves around the hummock where I sat so innocently vulnerable, and I span around, half-expecting to see them stealthily approaching from behind. But there was nothing."

The room was silent; even our shadows didn't move under the lamplight. My eyes shot to the corner, remembering how I had seen Mangitak's shape sliding back down the snow.

"He waved his arms," I told Pitseolak, "got up and walked steadily back towards where I was sitting on the skidoo. The wolves had gone down to the ice, he told me, and we both went to the top of the rise and looked down. The tracks petered out, heading in the direction of the old sunken boat. Your brother, it seems, had followed the marks for a couple of hundred yards. He said these were the same two wolves that had been seen by hunters some time before. Their den, apparently, was right across the sea ice, somewhere on Mallik Island.

"And so we went home. And that's the end of that!" I spoke with finality and we were both again back in the warmth of the living room, Pitseolak smiling, rubbing his hands — pleased, somehow grateful, as if he had just heard a tale of great daring told by some renowned hunter from the savannahs of Africa.

Yet the whole story was fairly ordinary in terms of the Arctic, not the type of adventure that was likely to be told over and over in years to come. I was initially surprised at Pitseolak's excitement, at his eagerness to hear details that were surely familiar to all Inuit — until I realized that they were not familiar to him. This barren country, which should have been his home, had become a foreign land.

"I've never seen a wolf in the snows," he said reflectively. "I think that you were both brave to go after them like that." He paused to think of them rummaging underneath his own house while he slept in ignorance a foot overhead. "If they had come to you, while my brother was away from the skidoo, you would have shot at them. I think you would have hit one of them and frightened them both away." He spoke as one trying to give comfort to an unwilling hero.

"I guess I would have," I replied. But in the clear setting of loneliness, without knowing anything about the speed or tactics of two wolves, I still had my own suspicions and recurring nightmares about what really would have happened.

"Could I have some tea, please," Pitseolak was asking.

"Sure. I'll put the kettle on."

I always served tea with what might be regarded as English exactitude: on a tray, sugar bowl, milk jug, and a plate of biscuits. Pitseolak expected it — it was part of his southern schooling. He invariably ate two or three biscuits only, placed his cup and saucer back carefully, and then wiped his mouth on a white handkerchief which he then replaced in his pocket. We indulged in the ceremony in virtual silence.

"Down at Fort Churchill," I asked when we were finished, "you do get polar bears, don't you?"

"Yes, they usually migrate southwards at a certain time of the year when it gets colder. We used to see them coming around the school compound. There was a general rubbish tip nearby, and they'd often come foraging around it for food."

"I read recently, in the *Eastern Arctic Newsweek*, that a student had been attacked and killed."

Pitseolak looked at me with surprise. "When was that?"

"I don't know exactly, but it was in a recent edition of the paper."

"Do you have a copy to hand?" he asked. I picked it up from the nearby bookshelf and found the appropriate page. He read the short article with interest.

"That's very unusual," he said. "The school staff was very cautious about things like that. We always knew when there were polar bears around. They made the tip area prohibited."

"Out of bounds," I corrected without intention.

"Yes, out of bounds." He thought for a while and then

said: "There was an occasion once when I was there when a boy nearly got too close to a polar bear on the tip — but he quickly ran back and leapt over the wire fencing. Some boy from Keewatin somewhere! They are certainly dangerous things, you know. A bit like the wolf, I suppose. If they are ever seen, or let themselves be seen, then it is because they are desperate for food."

"What was it like at Churchill?" I asked purposefully. I had long wanted to know about that school, but had become doubly interested since my friendship with Pitseolak.

He laughed, squeezed his hands, and raised his arms high over his head. He combed his fingers through the sides of his hair and grinned.

"It's a nice place, really. They have a dormitory for you to sleep in and they give you meals each day in a large sort of canteen. The staff are mainly very nice — although there was one of them, I can't remember his name, who didn't like me."

"That's almost to be expected," I offered in defence of the unknown aggressor. "You can't expect everyone to like everyone."

"No, I suppose not. But this teacher didn't like me. I know it."

"What sort of lessons did you have?"

"Well, we did most of the usual school things. You know...reading, writing, arithmetic...and all of those things. Of course, it was always in English. We also did some practical things like learning how to repair a skidoo, and art, and making things with wood."

"Did you like it there?" I asked.

"Sometimes I did. Other times, not. They had some silly rules about having to be inside the hostel at a certain time at night. And you couldn't go to other places without special permission. You know, they didn't like you to go to the local drinking places in case you got drunk or met some of the bad people of Churchill. But, of course, we used to manage to go off for a drink almost whenever we wanted to. I even got myself drunk one night — and I had to stay in and do extra work as a punishment."

"Really, when you think about it, the rules aren't that unusual," I said. "I mean, those are the sort of things which most boarding schools have to enforce."

"Oh, I know that. But I often felt that sometimes the teachers there were doing all those things to us because we were Eskimos. That they felt we couldn't be trusted. That we couldn't take liquor and didn't know how to behave. I know some of the men there didn't like us Eskimos!"

I found this hard to accept, and decided to change the subject.

"But do you think that having had the chance to go to Churchill has helped you? Haven't you benefited from it all? I mean, your English for example is excellent."

"Oh yes, I am pleased in a way that I did go there. I had the chance to see some of the bigger cities of Canada, and we used to take trips to museums and places like that. I enjoyed all of those things."

"In what ways was it all so bad, then?"

Pitseolak hesitated, as if reluctant to proceed. A smirk lodged itself obliquely across his mouth and he gazed at the carpet. After a fairly lengthy pause, he said, "You know, I picked up some bad habits from there. I got drunk and we used to gamble a lot with the workmen down there."

"But, let's be honest, there is a lot of gambling going on right here in Cape Dorset!" Constant card games seemed to be taking place in certain people's houses. In some houses, old ladies appeared to play from sun-up to sundown, as it were, using one-cent and five-cent pieces. Elsewhere, groups huddled over well-worn packs of cards, tossing dollar bills of all denominations onto the floor — in a manner reminiscent of the fabled Gold Rush days.

"You can't honestly say that you'd never gambled before," I said to Pitseolak.

"No, I know that I have. But there, in Churchill, it all seemed to be different. Men shouted and were violent with each other just because they had got the wrong cards in the deal. There was something almost frightening about watching those people playing cards. It was as if it wasn't just a game. When we play cards, like in Ooshooarlee's house, we know that someone will win and that others will lose. We accept this, and we play the game knowing that some will lose — maybe a lot of money. But down there they seem to get upset and violent if they lose." He looked at me, hoping that I could appreciate the different attitudes that he was desperately trying to convey. In a way, I did.

"I once had a fight with a boy at school, over cards," he said. "This is very bad. We usually don't fight like that, over such things. You see, there were lots of things like that which I saw at Churchill, which I do not think are good. And then there were lots of girls and women in that place who were very bad." He hesitated. "Do you know what I mean?"

"Yes, I know what you mean. But I am told that those things also go on in Frobisher Bay."

"But Frobisher Bay is not really an Eskimo town. It is a town made up by the Americans when they had some sort of base there. The Eskimos who live there are not like true Eskimos. They are all mixed up. They don't come from just one band or group. They are there for work, and they take on the ways of the kadloona until they don't even think like Eskimos any more!"

"But how do Eskimos really think, Pitseolak?" I asked, perhaps somewhat aggressively.

He didn't say anything. He sat silently, fingers stroking the furrows in his corduroy trousers, a tightly clenched fist tapping on the arm of the chair. He shifted his feet, stretched a leg, and then stared at me straight in the face.

"I don't know," he said finally. "That's the whole point. I don't know how Eskimos think!" I noticed that there were tears in his eyes. He lowered his head into his cupped hands and cried.

I left the room quietly. When I returned he had gone.

Six

Next day, I called in at the office of the Department of Northern Affairs to find out what had transpired from Pitseolak's visit and what his prospects of a job were. Also, I thought it might help if I put in a good word for him with the resident administrator.

George was a giant of a man, a lumberjack with a white and bushy hair-do to match his flowing chest-length beard. When I spoke, his kindly face expanded like a great balloon, then instantly collapsed into a shrivelled apple.

"Who?" he barked, lips pursed and rounded, eyebrows dropping into a quizzical frown.

"Pitseolak," I repeated.

"Never heard of him!" It wasn't a reflection of George's ignorance nor of any disinterest in his work; he had only been in the settlement a couple of weeks and one couldn't expect him to have become fully acquainted with everyone in such a short time. I explained who Pitseolak was and my reasons for sending him down for a talk, but it was more than evident that my highly recommended protegé had been nowhere near the building.

We discussed the problem of the deculturalized and, for the most part, unemployed young people who had been educated in government schools. George was entirely sympathetic, and from time to time he made a few random jottings on a long, yellow, legal pad, promising to take the issue up with his superiors when he filed his next monthly report.

"I'll do what I can," he offered helpfully. "The least I can do is to raise the problem with my boss and see what they're doing about it in other settlements. I imagine that it must be happening elsewhere too, not just here."

"And Pitseolak?" I asked.

"Sure. Send him down or bring him along yourself, and I'll see what we can do for him."

"Best if he comes alone," I countered. "Give me a specific time, and I'll make sure he comes this time."

George threw his hands slightly into the air, his eyes dancing across the wide desk at a scattering of typed sheets, booklets, and notes. "Half-nine in the morning?"

"Can't think that he'll have any other appointments at that time," I joked, getting to my feet and extending a hand. "Thanks a lot, George, for your time and help. I appreciate it."

With that, I left his cluttered office, pausing in the entranceway to browse through the neatly tacked rows of official circulars. One block told of current health hazards, birth-control programmes, and the times of the clinic in Frobisher Bay. There was a graphic document illustrating the dangers of botulism caused by eating decayed meat, which was a local delicacy; across the bottom was drawn a prone Eskimo figure, quite dead, a mystical cross hovering overhead in a puffy cloud. I glanced through a cluster of "official appointments" and at the list of government vacancies — teaching posts...housing officer for Igloolik... nurse for Pangnirtung. Then I left.

I reached home just as a bowl of soup was being lowered onto the table, and on my way across the room I picked up the walkie-talkie unit from the top of the bookcase. By arrangement of long standing with the Co-op manager, who was also the local postmaster and owner of the other part of the set, we made contact each day at exactly twelve-thirty. It was partially to chat and exchange news but also so that he could let me know of any flights that might be imminent, in case I wanted to dispatch newscasts to Frobisher Bay.

I gave the customary bleep-bleep at the precise moment and was soon cracking jokes with the postmaster. But after a few minutes, when I depressed my switch, there was a temporary silence at the other end. I tried again but got the same silence. Then I heard another voice — talking about sending a taxi for a passenger.

"Where is that exactly, dispatch?" came one speaker.

"Two blocks down east on Washington; three up to Lexicon. Number 3246, that is thirty-two forty-six. Can't miss it — a doctor's sign hanging right outside."

"Roger, dispatch. I'm on my way."

I couldn't believe it.

"What the heck was that?" I shouted into the black plastic mouthpiece as soon as the conversation was over.

"You heard it, too?" the postmaster replied with a laugh. "It's some taxi firm down in Montana. I was listening to it earlier."

"But that's light years away!"

"Yes. Freak waves drifting in our direction. I've heard them before." He paused and then proceeded, "No planes is no news. Sorry. What's happening your end?"

My end was barely a quarter of a mile away on the other side of a low-lying ridge. I could see his house from where I sat scooping luke-warm soup. My spindly aerial was aimed at his front window — we were only guaranteed a range of seven miles over the flat.

"Tell me," I began, "got any jobs going up for grabs over there in the print shop, or something like that? Got a man here who wants work and speaks excellent English."

"Obviously isn't you then," he gibed. "Who you got in mind, not that there's a single thing at present."

"Pitseolak — Oshoochiak's son. I thought you might be able to use him somehow or other and do both of you a good turn."

He hesitated and then replied, "Pitseolak! He's not very reliable you know. Likely as not, he'd come the first day or so and then start taking time off so that he can recover from a night out with the girls."

"Come off it! He's not that bad, and he really does seem in earnest about getting some work. Seriously, are you sure you've got nothing going?"

"No, sorry. Really, there is absolutely nothing at all. I couldn't even make up a job for him to do — but I'll keep him in mind when we come to do stocktaking later this month."

It was an obvious blank. A shot in the hopeful dark. We chatted for a while longer, arranged to meet for supper at the weekend, and then signed off.

Pitseolak came around that evening, reporting that he'd had no luck with job-hunting at the Bay. He was visibly depressed and it did little to cheer him up when I mentioned my own lack of success at the Co-op.

"I was planning to go there tomorrow," he said idly.

He massaged his face with fully stretched fingers and sighed. I had not seen him quite like this before — he was down and out.

"Hey! What happened with DNA?" I asked. "You didn't even poke your nose through the door to pass the time of day!"

He exhaled slowly again. Fed up. Weary.

"I forgot!" he snapped, then hastily admitted, "Actually, I didn't even bother. It's all such a waste of time. There's nothing happening around here, and I know it."

"Oh, come on, Pitseolak! You just can't give up like that. What on earth are you going to do with your life for the next sixty-odd years? Nothing? Keep borrowing money, with no hope in sight?"

"No, I think I'll walk around talking to myself in English all the time." It was bitterly said. He scratched the top of his head, then carefully replaced the ruffled strands of his quiff into their rightful place. "Man, I'm pissed off!" he said sullenly, slowly twisting his head from side to side. He obviously was.

An unfamiliar mood of gloom prevailed between us. It was unlike Pitseolak to be so negative. But as I sat there, mentally checking off the few jobs that he might do, I had to dismiss each in turn. Either they were unsuitable or there were no vacancies. Then, suddenly, I had an idea. "What about making work for ourselves?" I said. "I don't mean anything like setting up a window-cleaning business — or a house painting company — although, now that I say it, that's not quite so preposterous. But let's try to create something ourselves that will provide you with regular work, alongside some of your friends."

He was interested, but slightly confused. "What have you got in mind? A factory for canning arctic char?"

"All right, let's not be cynical! At least hear me out."

"Sorry."

"How about setting up a newspaper?" I paused to let the idea sink in. In point of truth, I had been toying with the scheme for months and had even corresponded with a couple of editors from other settlements. I sifted some samples from a pile of documents on the side table and dropped them in Pitseolak's lap. "Why not do the same here?" I said.

He flicked through the shallow wad of duplicated pages, hesitating now and then to read a specific item. At least the act of reading these amateur efforts was stimulating his attention. He turned one page sideways to look at a drawing, then turned it right again before allowing the other pages to glide quickly through his fingers.

"Nobody could make any money at it at first, but at least it would keep quite a few of us busy," I explained.

"Could be." He was nibbling the bait, then finally he grasped the hook: "But what do we write about? Where do we get the news? Who does the writing? Is it in English or Eskimo, or both? We'd need help. Where do we get the paper? How do we duplicate it?" His mind rushed, questions flowing like waters cascading over the rapids of a young effervescent stream.

"Hold it!" I stopped his encouraging flurry of questions. "First of all, what about it, as an idea?"

"Got possibilities," he admitted, his thoughts still racing ahead. "At least keep us occupied for a while!"

"All right, then. Let's think about it first of all, quite carefully. No point in charging ahead on the spur of the moment, then forgetting about it tomorrow. Leave production problems to me, for the time being. You simply go away and let the whole idea turn over in your mind. Ask others what they think about the idea of having a local newspaper, and then, if there's even the slightest glimmer of interest, start thinking along more serious lines. Will it just be local news, or should we include information and facts about other settlements too? Do we want controversial items relating to Eskimos and Northern Development? What about snippets of news on international affairs — do we include these?"

I paused before the entire list of considerations became too overpowering for both of us. Then I continued, "You'd become the editor, so perhaps you could also scout around and see if you can enlist some of your mates to become reporters and the suchlike. We might involve about half a dozen others if we eventually settled on a weekly publication."

He jumped to his feet, fired by motive for the first time in a long while. "I'll go and see Aitee, Nowdla, and some of the others and see what they think. Aitee's good at writing stories." He dressed rapidly and was soon sliding out amongst the snowbanks. As I watched him, I suddenly remembered his appointment with George next morning.

"Don't forget this time!" I shouted after him through the crisp, calm air. "Nine-thirty sharp!"

He raised an arm in acknowledgement, swiftly jerking it in the manner he had learnt from watching a TV Western series: "I'm from Wells Fargo, mam!"

Three hours later he was back, just as enthused and with several others in tow. Together, we discussed the outlines of the scheme and settled on a preliminary format that included alternating columns in both languages. Nowdla agreed to do the translating, and between us various other areas of responsibility were sorted out and accepted.

If the venture was destined to fail before it ever really got started, then a fair portion of the blame was mine. I had severely underestimated the availability of materials and the amount of time required to order replacements. The school was willing to grant us the use of a duplicator but was reluctant to commit its own limited fund of fluid in case it ran short later in the term. Similarly, DNA was willing to supply the paper, at no charge for the first edition, but could not be sure of taking delivery of actual stock for the next two or three months.

"It's a great idea," offered George, "but let's get it all going for the next fiscal year when I'll be able to make proper allowances in the budget." Bare practicalities had burst our balloon.

Needless to say, George had not been able to offer Pitseolak a job with DNA, though Pitseolak had at least kept the appointment and had had quite a long talk with George — or so I gathered. Something might come of it, though I was not very hopeful. And, in the meantime, we were back at stage one — except that Pitseolak's brief foray into journalism had restored his spirits. It was he who suggested that we form a table tennis club. Still riding on the wave of our recent enthusiasm, we quickly organized a night and a venue. Nowdla undertook to sell sodas and chocolate, and we arranged a knock-out tournament involving roughly thirty participants. Although we had started by heading in one direction, we had ended up facing another. But at least the weeks would now have some sort of purpose, and it was a relief to see Pitseolak laughing and smiling again. He would take his role as club president seriously, I felt sure.

But the ship had only just been saved before its disillusioned crew abandoned it. It was difficult to know how long we could keep it afloat before it was lost again in the troubled seas of despair.

Seven

"There once was a time when Ataksak lived in heaven, with brightly coloured cords hanging from his clothes and whose death was always seen by a radiant shining in the skies. During this same time, Oluksak lived along the banks of the rivers and lakes, giving personal inspiration to the spiritual leaders of the people. Across the naked earth, one could sometimes see the scurrying figure of a hairless dog. This was Keelut, the omen of evil."

"How do you know about these things?" Pitseolak seemed fascinated. He was sitting on the couch in the living room.

"Because I am interested," I replied curtly, without intending it.

"But why do you bother to find out about all of this?"

"Because you don't know about it, do you? And nobody else seems to care around here either."

"No, but then these are things from the past. They're myths. Why should I bother about them?"

"That's the whole point, Pitseolak!" I leaned forward, challenging his naivety. "Don't you see? These are the sorts of things that helped to make your entire culture so unique. Stories, or myths if you like, such as these set you apart from so many other cultures. And now you, an Eskimo, tell me that you've never heard of any of it! You even ask me why it matters! Don't you realize that your whole culture is collapsing around you — and no one is even showing willing to capture the vital threads before they disappear completely?''

"Well, when it comes down to it, why should we? We've long since abandoned all of that. We became Christians long ago. So who cares about Keelut the dog or those others you mentioned a short while ago.''

"But aren't you at least curious to know a little bit about your history and what went on up here before we kadloonas popped up and started to change it all?''

"Of course, it's interesting," he conceded. "But then I do know something about our past. I've read all about Martin Frobisher, Baffin, Button, Bylot, and the rest. They made maps, which we had never bothered to do; they gave us guns and all of those other things that have helped make life easier. Hudson's Bay gave us somewhere to sell seal skins, to buy and trade for the things we need." He grinned and then impishly added, "They gave us the money that we need to send off to Eaton's for the clothes and other things we want.''

"Rubbish, Pitseolak!" I laughed. "And you know it! You know what I'm talking about — I'm talking about a culture, your culture, which is rapidly falling to pieces around us. At this very moment, while we are sitting here on nylon-covered, foam-padded cushions, the whole thing is collapsing. And all you can say is 'so what?' ''

"But this is reality, isn't it?" he asked hesitantly. "Sure, the Eskimo way of life is changing. But is it that bad? Aren't they all much better off with all of these things?" He waved an arm around the room.

I couldn't help noticing that he was using "them" and "they," as if he had nothing to do with these people at all, wasn't even one of them himself.

"But aren't you just a little bit curious about your ancestors?"

"Why?" he asked. "What does the past really matter?"

I shook my head, glancing up towards a crack in the ceiling.

"Well, Pitseolak, at least that shows some indication that you are at least part Eskimo, after all."

"Why?" he asked, chuckling at his half-caste status.

"Because I get the constant impression that Eskimos are primarily concerned only with today. Where's the food? Where are the caribou? What can I do today? Everything is for today — not yesterday which has gone, not tomorrow which may never come. Forever today and never the future."

He cupped his hands, blew an owl's hoot through the two bent thumbs and remarked, "I'm obviously an exception then, because I am thinking about the future at this very moment. And the not-so-distant future. I'm off to Alert."

"You're what?"

"I'm off to Alert," he repeated through the whiteness of a smug grin. "I had a long talk to DNA. Then spent some time thinking about what courses they had going and were willing to send me on. Then I decided to become an engineer — a mechanic, fixing generators and bulldozers, that sort of thing."

"That's fantastic! But you sure picked some fine time to tell me. There was I trying desperately to resurrect your culture — and out of the blue you announce that you're off, away from the whole thing!" I paused to reorientate my own thinking. "When do you go?"

He crossed his legs, removing a piece of stray cotton that had fastened itself to the toe of his brightly coloured nylon stretch socks.

"First of all, in a few days' time probably, I'm going to Frobisher for a quick course. This should last about two weeks, he thinks — George that is. Then I'll come back here for a while and get my things ready and packed. Should be off to Alert next month sometime."

It had seemed to be such a short while ago that we were trying to plot his future, but now it was evident that all of the disjointed parts had suddenly dropped into place. He had decided, with remarkable ease apparently, what he wanted to do. A mechanic! The word had never even entered into our conversations. In fact, he had at one stage indicated that he wasn't that way inclined. But here it all was, the last key, a target to aim for — though I did wonder whether he mightn't have grabbed just as quickly at the chance to train as a potter or newscaster had the options been presented.

"What's Alert got to do with it?" I asked, still a trifle taken aback by the entire revelation.

"Oh, that's just a place where I can go to get experience." He tossed it nonchalantly. "Seems they're always wanting people up there. Because it's so remote and out of the way, they have a problem getting volunteers to go there. The money's good, though, and plenty of opportunity to learn the job because there's nothing else to do."

He paused, glanced at his watch and observed, "Hey, time for 'The Northern Messenger' isn't it? Let's see how that man at Port Burwell is making out with his letters to his wife."

I turned the knob obligingly. There was never any need to tune the radio set, as this was the only programme we were ever certain of receiving. Sure enough, the announcer's voice began to crackle forth, sending an assortment of personal messages.

"Are you absolutely certain about all this, Pitseolak?" I asked as he leaned forward, listening eagerly to the announcer rustling through the papers of the next letter to be read over the air.

Pitseolak jerked his attention away from the black and white dial of the radio, almost as if he was annoyed at the interruption. "Sure! Sure, I'm sure!" he replied, slightly irritated.

"What does your father think about the whole scheme?"

"Oh, he thinks it's a great idea. Says he'll miss me, of course, but then admits that at least it's a chance to do something useful and to learn a trade that I'll always be able to use. There'll always be jobs in the settlements, although naturally I'd want to come back here to work and live."

He sharply turned back to the radio, exclaiming at the same time, "Hey! This is for you!"

We peered into the glass frontage, as if expecting something or someone to appear on its nonexistent screen. Along the airwaves came that old familiar voice. It was undoubtedly for me: "The cat is fine and sleeps on our bed. Zeki is getting fatter so we have put her on a diet. Everything else around here is fine and everyone says to say hello." There was a pause: "The next letter is for Fred and Willie up there in Clyde River...."

"The cat's fine," I repeated, embarrassed. "At least we've learned that much about the events of the world."

"Who's Zeki, or Zaki?" Pitseolak asked with genuine concern.

"The dog," I replied with slow deliberation, feeling foolish.

"Oh, I see." He really did seem to be interested.

I stood up and went into the kitchen, the story of somebody's grandmother's carnations drifting gently across the room and into Pitseolak's attentive ears.

"Coffee?" I shouted.

"Please!" he called back, and I left him happily engaged in this public eavesdropping on other people's lives. The dog is on a diet; how utterly absurd.

Pitseolak was still avidly listening to the set when I returned, and I watched him curiously, thinking of our earlier discussion about Inuit myths. We were in a strange situation. While I was fast becoming obsessed with a desire to learn all that I could about his culture, he was just as eagerly leaping into mine. We were passing each other in midstream, going in opposite directions. But I couldn't be quite sure which one of us was the defector.

When the broadcast had finished and all of its earth-shattering trivia had been disclosed, I broached the subject again: "I still find it odd that you don't appear to know much about your own old way of life, and that you're not even interested in it."

Pitseolak put down his cup and wiped his mouth with a handkerchief. Meticulously, he folded it back into the carefully ironed creases and then looked at me thoughtfully. "Perhaps I am interested sometimes," he conceded with calculated care. "After all, I do feel a bit silly when someone asks me a question which they presume I can answer — and I can't." He curled his bottom lip and then moistened it with the top one. "But the simple truth is that I've never heard of this hairless dog you mentioned earlier — Keelut or whatever you called it. And, also, remember that I've never really been hunting, other than odd short trips many years ago. You see, although I was born an Eskimo, I actually know less about many of their ways than you do. Strange, but true. In some senses, all of the schooling has made me into more of a kadloona. To be honest, I only ever feel that I am Eskimo when I am up here and with my family."

I stroked my beard with an open palm. I didn't want to hurt his feelings after this frank confession of his ignorance, but I did want to tell him more of the things that I was finding so increasingly fascinating. It was as if I felt some inner compulsion to share this knowledge which I was so deliberately acquiring, to pass it on before it was too late.

"Did you know that something was seen right here in Cape Dorset not that long ago that could very well have been Keelut?"

He bulged his eyes and his mouth fell slightly open with surprise.

"Do what?" he said, startled.

"I said that it is quite possible that this mythical creature called Keelut was seen here quite recently. In fact, a member of your very own family told me about it last week. He didn't actually use the name Keelut, but what he described was a strange dog, which, oddly enough, appeared shortly after the death of the last great local man of mystery."

Pitseolak's earlier reaction had matured into one of astonishment. He half-smiled, as if he thought I was having him on. He was certainly intrigued — partly because he hadn't heard of the incident to which I so obliquely referred, and doubly so because a member of his own family had told me, without ever mentioning it to him. Had he really become such an outsider?

"What the heck are you talking about?" he challenged. But he was curious.

I stretched my legs, flexed the ankles, and rolled back into the softness of the chair.

"You've obviously heard of Kingwatchiak?" I began. It was rhetorical. Most males born in the year of his death carried his name. "Well, it would appear that not only was he a great leader of the people here but that he was also different from them in other respects. A bit like a shaman, or witch doctor, that the Indians have. I must admit that whenever I've tried to ask about this part of his personality, most of my informants tend to appear to be daft! Anyhow, one night when most people were at the Community Hall for a dance or something like that, he died. A fire, I believe, destroyed his home with him inside." Pitseolak fixed his eyes firmly and intently on mine. He didn't flinch.

"Now, as I told you, before it was known beyond doubt that he was well and truly dead, a white dog was seen walking across the snow towards the mountain. It was a bit like a large fox, had a long tail. As described to me by several different eyewitnesses, it was walking very slowly, its tongue hanging out and panting. Furthermore, it is generally agreed that this doglike creature was so bright and white that it was sort of glowing."

"What happened when it got to the mountain?"

"You could ask your own brother. He told me that he saw it. He said he watched it for a few minutes. It had short legs and went very, very slowly across the snows. But it didn't reach the mountain. Instead, it just disappeared and the peculiar glow faded away."

Pitseolak was silent. Impressed and amazed, but also confused.

After a while, he asked, "What do you think it was?"

"I've absolutely no idea whatsoever! I've merely told you what I have been told. But I do happen to believe your brother when he tells me that he is convinced he did see something. And his own description of this weird dog is consistent with other descriptions — I've even got a drawing of it that he did for me. Also, I took the trouble to go to the house where he and two others say they saw the creature from, and the descriptions they gave of its path over the snow certainly fit the view from that house.

"But the whole point really is that here was an old man, maybe a rather strange and mysterious old man at that, whose death coincided with the claimed sighting of a strange glowing dog. All I want to say to you, Pitseolak, is that this was an incident that occurred recently — right on your own doorstep, as it were — and that it's remarkably similar to the old traditional Eskimo myth about the hairless dog Keelut, the omen of evil."

"Why do you say that Kingwatchiak was a mysterious man?" Pitseolak interrupted.

"Let's get this straight! I didn't say he was. He said it himself. He quite openly claimed to possess strange powers and reputedly once declared that these powers would be seen by others when he died." Pitseolak bowed his head. Like me, he didn't understand the story and was fascinated.

"Anyhow, don't expect me to give you the answers to the whole business. I'm only repeating the things I've been told by some of the people around here whose opinions I happen to respect. But what I am saying is that perhaps your own culture — and it is part of you whether you feel part of it or not — is quite interesting, to say the least."

For some time Pitseolak didn't say anything. He was picturing this awesome animal ambling across the snow, his own brother watching its panting path. I sensed, too, that he was wondering why they had chosen to tell me — and not him.

"I wonder what it was?" he asked vacantly.

"Search me!" Then, in the hope that he might be able to clear up any doubts he had, I suggested that he check it all out for himself.

"Ask around and see who else saw it. At least that will give you something useful to do with yourself, instead of lying in bed all day waiting to go off to Frobisher!" I poked his foot playfully. The conversation had pleasantly completed a full circle. And I was pleased that he was now aware not only of his own future but also of the existence of a past.

Eight

On Friday, 14 March, Pitseolak left for Frobisher Bay to take the preliminary course connected with his mechanic's training in Alert.

"I'm on my way up the ladder now," he remarked as he walked towards the waiting aircraft. "I'm on my way up!"

"Can't go up much farther than Alert," I added dryly. And he took off.

I had never thought that Jill and I would miss him quite as much as we did. Although he was only away for a couple of weeks, his absence left a curious void. We had grown accustomed to his cheery face and lively conversation, and I, in particular, had always enjoyed the hours which had been so interestingly whiled away over innumerable cups of coffee and tea. I felt as if our conversation had been broken off in mid-sentence, for neither of us had satisfactorily been able to answer many of the questions that had been raised during our chats. I recalled asking Pitseolak how Eskimos thought, and he had frankly admitted to not knowing. But, there again, how indeed did they really think? What was it that made them think in such a different manner? Why was it that they lived a life so elegantly embroidered with unchallenged stories about one another? How different was life in the open tundra, when you came down to it, from settlement life? What did it do to a person to have to live day to day on skill alone, when conditions made food such a precarious commodity?

It was to satisfy my curiosity, as much as for the sake of adventure, that I took advantage of the opportunity to go off hunting with Pitseolak's brother Mangitak. He had suggested it long ago, joking that I would be shooting with a camera and he would be shooting with a rifle. But arranging it all proved to be far more complex than I had imagined.

From the outset, long before we ever headed out into the wide white beyond, I found myself confronted with a case of the most extraordinary frustration, which was itself born of our conflicting cultural philosophies. By habit, I make arrangements or appointments in advance and then do my utmost to adhere to them right down to the smallest details. Not so with my intended companions, whose inherent awareness of the uncertainty of survival tended to make them, at least superficially, quick deciders rather than long-range planners.

"When can we go hunting?" I had asked Mangitak.

"I don't know," came the reply.

"This week?"

"Eemaha. Maybe."

"Tomorrow?"

"Eemaha."

"What time?"

"I don't know," with a long shrug of the shoulders.

"Eight in the morning?"

"Eemaha."

"Who else will go?" I knew that hunters always went in pairs.

"I don't know."

"Tytoosie?"

"Maybe. Eemaha."

"If it happens that we do go tomorrow, possibly at eight

in the morning, and if Tytoosie is coming, will he come up here to join us?"

"I don't know."

I paused to take a deep breath and tried to piece the jigsaw of the plan into one sentence speckled with the correct vagaries: "If it so happens that we can go tomorrow, at eight in the morning, and if Tytoosie is coming to meet us up here — if he is coming that is — then tell him that I'll buy the skidoo gas and bullets. That is, if we go."

Mangitak smiled. We were obviously going, as so circuitously established, but the verbal roundabout on which we had been spinning was an instinctive acknowledgement of the unpredictability of the future — even a future that by then was only twelve hours away. Mangitak was unable to commit himself because of this inbred notion of fatalism.

It was, therefore, with some degree of relief that I awoke the following morning to find Tytoosie's long wooden sled parked outside the door. Soon afterwards, Mangitak appeared and carefully and thoughtfully began to pack the supplies that we would be needing during the course of what seemed likely to be many days in the spaciousness of the tundra. I went outside.

"So, we're off?" I began optimistically.

"Eemaha." We were back in the old routine.

"What time is Tytoosie coming up?"

"I don't know."

"Possibly about an hour?" I had already been sitting with an uncomfortable amount of clothing on for some considerable time and longed to be able to peel off several layers if there were to be more hours of waiting.

"How long are we going for?"

"I don't know." Which of course was quite true, since it all depended on what was caught and how far away we would have to go. Obviously, Mangitak didn't know how long we would be gone.

Since he wouldn't let me help him pack the sled — I clearly knew little about weight and balance for such a vehicle bouncing across the ice — I decided to go back inside where it would at least be warmer. I guessed that maybe, eemaha, we would leave within the hour. So I heated some soup and decided to remove one of the layers of clothing that had so successfully managed to give me a Herculean physique; but I dropped the clothes by the doorway so as not to delay our departure a second more than necessary. Within five minutes, bowl of soup in hand, I wandered from the kitchen into the living room to watch Mangitak loading up. But he wasn't there! Come to that, neither was the sled. They had gone. Without me.

Now, there have been noted historians who have gone on record as claiming that empires were won through determination. If this be true, then I fled the house like Alexander the Great, hitching up my braces and trying to put on the second of two enormous caribou mittens which the local missionary had loaned me. But running along the ruts made by the runners of the big komatik was far from simple. My legs wouldn't bend at the knees for they were clad in a pair of long johns, a tracksuit, a pair of trousers, and a preposterous pair of bulky pantaloons made from caribou fur which a neighbour had thoughtfully lent me that same morning. Rather than run, I was thus compelled to adopt a gait best described as an urgent waddle — all of which helped to make me even more conspicuous as I hurried after the sled through the awakening settlement.

I finally saw the hunting party below the Bay store, down on the ice, and only by taking a short cut across the snow-covered rocks did I manage to catch them up beyond the ridges. I was exhausted.

"Why didn't you tell me you were going?" I gasped, annoyed.

"I thought that maybe you'd changed your mind," Mangitak replied.

"That's ridiculous!" I laughed, clambering aboard the polar-bear-skin pad that he had built for my sitting comfort.

"It is possible," Mangitak said. "Here, anything is possible." And off we bounced, Tytoosie's skidoo leading the way.

To say that I was even remotely relaxed would be to tell a lie. What with the freezing wind relentlessly pounding into my face and the unceasing jerks, bangs, and thumps that the sled made, I quickly learned to keep my thoughts on the basic need to hold onto the ropes for dear life. Mangitak was steering the skidoo that was towing me, and I felt he would be unlikely to notice if I fell off — a prospect that held little appeal for me. It seemed to be ages before he eventually did turn round, by which time my feet were without perceptible sensations, a fact that I managed to convey through a miscellany of one-handed waves and gestures. He stopped immediately, leapt off and ran back; then, with the expertise of an attendant in a highly expensive massage parlour, he stripped my feet and gently rubbed back the tingling feelings which I'd thought had gone for ever.

"We stop whenever we feel cold," he remarked. "It doesn't matter how often. We always stop, because if the cold goes too deep then maybe we will freeze altogether." It was an ominous, logical thought.

After a hastily brewed cup of tea, we continued on our way, bouncing and jerking over the frozen surface, the runners of the sled shearing their way through the natural silence. It was a moonscape where nothing moved and no one lived. Whenever we paused, all went quiet and motionless again.

The scenery was spectacular. There was none of the grandeur of the Himalayan peaks nor the extravagance of the Grand Canyon, and yet, in its monotonous simplicity, this scenery was somehow even more breath-taking. It was naked, raw, real. Not made for backdrops. Unseen by most of the world. It was honest, unpreened, a backwater of beauty, born of the ruthless parentage of present elements and ancient Ice Age.

We followed the flat sea ice and detoured along the bottoms of shallow valleys. On either side, gentle curves dominated the near and far horizons, their smoothness occasionally interrupted by a craggy boulder or a deep incision sliced into the fleshy snows, where underlying ice had slipped. The snow sprawled with that same firm silkiness and satisfaction that one finds when stroking the back of a responsive cat: down the head, along the spine, and up into the tail. It was solid and satisfying. Whiteness overpowered everything, yet there were also subtle shades of grey and blue which cast delicate shadows from behind boulders before disappearing into nothing. Sometimes an inookshook would rise incongruously from a low-lying summit, an assembly of laminated rocks, built to mark a route or to locate a strategic spot; it would watch us pass, like some frozen black scarecrow, and I too stared back until it was gone, its presence no longer felt.

We proceeded along the shoreline and then turned northwards up the Chorkbak Inlet, guiding the sleds through the awkward blocks of ice which the persisting tidal changes of a confused frozen sea had tossed hither and thither into a bewildered belt of rigid, broken waves. And then we climbed the snow-clad slopes of land once more and headed inland.

From time to time we would pass the remnants of an igloo made by some previous band of hunters, the spiralling sides abruptly curling towards the domed top which had long since been battered and destroyed into a vacant gaping hole. Around the bases were invariably the scuffle-marks of the marauding packs of wolves, who, with desperate hunger, had cleared the site of any traces of human refuse. They had always gone and we never saw them, only this evidence of their continual presence in the tundra — watching, looking, waiting somewhere else for the chance to attack or move in.

Mangitak and Tytoosie alternated in taking the lead, their faces serious and unflinching, eyes constantly moving, seeing everything, missing nothing; forever alert. They went as if by instinct, chasing a prey which neither had yet seen or even located but forging ahead with knowledgeable determination, buoyed by the confidence that this was their land too. Somewhere unknown would be a small herd of caribou, scratching for food among the buried grasses and lichen, ears twitching erect at the slightest sounds, muscles responsive and tense. In an hour, or a day or a week, they would be found; and they would die.

We stopped quite often for tea, taking advantage of these moments to jump about and to flex aching shoulders, backs, and knees. We would jog a little and circle arms until the body felt nearly well again, and then we would move off once more. It was a relentless pursuit, not a pleasant outing or a casual joy-ride, but a trip of necessity which would persist until the hunters had gathered enough food from this deserted garden.

The farther we travelled, the more conscious I became of my companions' confidence. We had no tents, nowhere to sleep, no heat — only what their skills could provide. If a skidoo broke down, we would have to rely solely on their ability to repair the part, correct the fault; there was no other help around, no spare-parts shop to fall back on, no hotel to retreat to if all else failed. Sitting on the sled, hour after hour, trying to repel the penetrating cold, I kept thinking of their brazen defiance, even when nature had stacked the odds against them. But I gradually came to appreciate that they had the right level of confidence and always retained sufficient respect for the unpredictable and unknown. Risks, playing the odds, these had no place in their mental armoury. They and endless generations of ancestors had survived not by chance but by wise contemplation and calculated actions. They knew their own limits, the true extent of their abilities, and made no attempt to exceed these. No challenges, just a cautious truce.

"How long could you last out here?" I asked Tytoosie during one of our rests. "Without a skidoo, sled, food, heat. All alone without any help. Nothing save perhaps a pocketknife."

He thought a moment, staring into the sparkling snow which would be his witness. "About three weeks," he replied without conceit. "Or perhaps longer." He paused, then added, "If you left me right here in this spot, I could get back to Cape Dorset and still survive about thirty-one days." We were already some hundred and fifty miles from the settlement, but I didn't doubt him.

"And me?" I asked hopefully.

"With absolutely nothing — just like you would have me — I think you would not last more than three hours." I didn't doubt this either.

Whenever we stopped, it was for a reason: we were tired or cold or thirsty. And when we came to the end of a day it was because we were hungry and sleepy. There was never any wasted time. Mangitak and Tytoosie could build an igloo in about twenty-five minutes, selecting the correct type of snow and then erecting the structure from these styrofoamlike blocks which cemented themselves together on contact. We would eat and then sleep — no sitting up half the night indulging in idle chatter. The igloo was functional, stark, for we had only stopped and built it for these two purposes. It wasn't particularly warm inside, about -10°F, though this was cosy compared to the -40°F outside. When we breathed, a thin layer of ice formed across the inside wall, making the snow house even more of a cocoon in which we had buried ourselves.

I found myself constantly watching these two hunters, trying to understand them, studying their actions and behaviour. They amazed and fascinated me, and it had long been apparent that their hunt would be successful.

One day we stopped on the fringes of Tessik Lake. It was the umpteenth tea break, and in order to add a dash of variety, I opened a tin of butter with the intention of furnishing a quick snack. The contents, separated into swirls of yellow and yellow ochre, had gone rancid.

"So much for my bright idea," I announced, waving the tin for Tytoosie to see. "It's a waste!"

"Nothing is ever a waste out here," he kindly admonished, snatching it from me.

As Mangitak melted the snow for our drink, Tytoosie ambled off some distance and placed the tin — about the size of a regular sardine tin — onto the ice. Neither time nor objects were to be wasted while he waited for his tea. He was going to practise his shooting. He took aim and then stopped.

"You," he gestured, proffering a rifle.

I shot at the distant tin and, of course, missed. Without practice, nobody ever improves, and I hadn't fired a rifle since I had so memorably missed the target at Christmas. My second bullet entered the barrel and then stuck halfway up. Mangitak belted the rifle against the snow a few times and then peered up the hole; then he clobbered it again against the runner of the sled before arriving at the conclusion that the bullet was firmly wedged. I had long been amazed at the casual way Eskimos seemed to treat their guns — none of the nightly greasing, polishing, and cleaning which my limited military exposure had suggested was vital. But now there was a dilemma: one of the essential weapons was out of action and it would have to be repaired.

It was remarkable to watch Tytoosie tackling the problem. I could all but swear to having heard his brain squirming as he held the offending rifle and looked about him for a solution. Even with a fully equipped workshop, it is far from easy to dislodge a stubborn bullet, and we had nothing whatsoever. Before my own guilt-ridden mind could begin to function, Tytoosie was standing by the sled, studying it, and removing one of the metal rings that had been used to help fasten the rope binding to the framework. He found the join, forced it open, and began to pound it with the butt of the damaged rifle. Gradually it opened wider and wider, getting flatter and flatter with each crashing thump until it was flat and fairly straight. I watched, mesmerized by his fast-thinking ingenuity. Then he placed the blade of his knife upright at one end and bashed that with the rifle butt until a slight indentation appeared. He stood up, saying nothing, eyes dancing with the excitement of the challenge, looking, searching for something else. He grabbed a rope, undid a single strand, and then tied it firmly around the end of the flattened ring so that it held fast within the tiny groove he had made with his knife blade.

For the next hour, we squatted in the snow, watching him as he patiently lowered and raised the device up and down the barrel. Tap-tap-tap. We sipped tea, watching until the bullet finally popped out. Tytoosie smiled, looked through the barrel, and then promptly inserted another bullet. Quickly, he swivelled around, squatting on one leg. He took aim, and a magnificent spray of rancid butter fountained into the air, the tin flickering light as it sped into the distance.

"Are we ready to go?" he asked Mangitak. The latter nodded and we clambered aboard once more. It was the first thing Tytoosie had said since asking me to take a potshot in the first place. Sometimes talking was a waste of time, too.

Hours later, bobbing up and down with increasing discomfort atop the komatik, I was still marvelling at the initiative of the man. Having nothing makes you think. With shops nearby and tools at hand, most of us have barely begun to tap our initiative. The Eskimo hunters have developed theirs to the utmost, out of sheer need. I looked around at the undulating whiteness. There was nothing, but I felt very secure.

It was several days before we encountered signs of the prey. Tytoosie leapt off his skidoo and was gently stroking some barely noticeable marks in the snow. Travelling at about 15 mph, it was a miracle that he had seen them in the first place. Standing still and looking intently at the tips of his fingers pointing at the snow, I still had difficulty in seeing anything.

"Five caribou," I heard him conferring with Mangitak, "were here three days ago. They are moving very slowly in that direction. We shall have them this afternoon." He explained this again to me, not knowing that I had already heard the pair of them discussing the tracks. "We shall catch them up in about three hours." He turned and was off again, engine revving with added incentive.

The markings became more obvious as we followed the trail, and even I could recognize them: footprints of one animal, then two, three, four; exposed tufts of greenery, half-chewed; soil kicked over where nothing had grown; the marks of an endless trek in search of food. We followed them until we came into a small basin. The machines had been hardly ticking over for the previous fifteen minutes, idling only enough to keep us moving and making no noise. We cruised to a silent stop.

"Up here! They're over here!" whispered Tytoosie. Both men grabbed rifles and crawled to the edge of the lip. We lay motionless, heads barely visible from the outside, and looked where Mangitak was pointing. There, several hundred yards away, were the predicted five caribou, a herd that had lagged behind the main migration. At first, they carried on pawing the snow, unconcerned, unknowing. Then, as the two hunters settled into their customary squatting firing stance, the animals became rigid, eyes swivelling and nostrils flexing to detect the unseen intrusion that they realized had infiltrated their peace. No shots were fired, there were no movements, just the inactive suspense of two parties in a pending battle, awaiting the correct moment to strike.

Then the stag leapt forward, the sign to the rest of the group to dart rapidly in the same direction. There was an explosion, and, with front legs still outstretched, its mighty antlers twisted ungainly, the magnificent creature dropped dead. The remaining caribou pranced in utter confusion, first this way, then that. Without a leader, they were robbed of direction and purpose. Mangitak and Tytoosie fired shot after shot. Within a minute, all was silent again. No one and nothing moved.

We stood up and walked down the outer edge of the basin, casually counting empty cartridge cases. With seven bullets, Tytoosie had shot four of the herd; with four bullets, Mangitak had claimed one. They agreed that they had not been wasteful.

Witnessing the slaughter from the crest five hundred yards away was quite a different experience from walking through the carnage site itself. Large eyes stared blankly through an encroaching glaze of freezing liquid, then became sinisterly white all over even as I was looking at them. Trickling blood froze onto the surface of the dense fur like rivers of brittle glass, and where it had dripped or sprawled onto the ice it soaked into pink patches. Clots congealed and set into grotesque shapes, shining and sparkling as if they were the creations of some bizarre sculptor of red crystal.

"Over here!" Mangitak was suddenly calling. I looked over my shoulder. He was beckoning me to come, cradling the head of one animal which was still very alive.

"You said that you wanted a close-up photograph of a live caribou," he remarked. "Tytoosie deliberately shot this one only in the leg. He did it for you. So, now you can take your picture."

I set the camera, adjusted the focus and saw the animal's quizzical eyes through the lens before firing the shutter. I didn't wait as Tytoosie dug the knife into the back of its neck, but I could hear him probing to locate the spinal cord.

"Why not shoot it?" I called. Tytoosie stood astride the frightened, kicking caribou, still cutting and digging for the right spot.

"Can't waste bullets," he replied. I might well have predicted the answer.

Nor did they waste time. It was far too cold. Using only conventional sheath knives, they skinned and jointed one caribou a piece within twenty minutes — legs, ribs, heads, livers, intestines laid in neat piles ready for packing onto the sled. As the wind whipped the snow into thrashing flurries, the day grew even colder, and whenever their bare, working hands became too cold, they plunged them eagerly into the pulpy bloody stomachs. Later, I would do the same.

The carefully folded animal skins became speckled with white. The meat was instantly frozen, seeming to want only plastic wrappers and printed price tags to make it look suitable for the display counters of a supermarket. The two men worked deftly, efficiently. The cuts they made were precise, and they dissected with the accuracy of a surgeon, knowing each fibre, muscle, and sinew. There was blood everywhere — on hands, clothing, and even on the sleds and skidoos which had somehow managed to get down here unseen by me. And the tea was already boiling.

"Get the beans on!" called Mangitak as he bent over to rip into the belly of another caribou.

"Try this instead!" shouted Tytoosie. He bit into a chunk of meat which he had just cut from the carcass scattered about his bloodied feet and tossed it to me. I gnawed a mouthful and threw it back. It was like trying to eat a fleshy ice-lolly, rather tasteless. But at least I knew that it was fresh. Very fresh.

I had never been so completely surrounded by such a gory mess before. In a way, I wanted to help Mangitak and Tytoosie, but I didn't have the slightest idea about what to do. They, in turn, appreciated this and were happy to let me do nothing.

Two hours later, having loaded the meat and finished a hot meal, we were already on our way back, following the same tracks and valleys that we had taken several days earlier. There was a sense of satisfaction, a feeling of joy that sometimes broke freely and openly into elation, laughter, and singing. But there was never carelessness or a diminishing of alertness. And when a stray husky pup came trotting from nowhere towards us, Tytoosie shot it through the head without even stopping his skidoo.

"Sometimes they are dangerous," he calmly explained.

That night, we lay in an igloo sipping tea. Our frozen breath and sweaty bodies made the atmosphere deceptively steamy — like a sauna. The bottom half of a caribou leg was being passed around, and we each took turns in biting mouthfuls of the raw meat which had become the main course for supper.

"I see that you still wonder about the husky," remarked Mangitak. I hadn't referred to it, knowing that for whatever reason there was, Tytoosie had been right to kill it. But I could still see it playfully romping towards us across the snow, as pleased to see us as a lost child finding its mother on a crowded beach.

"Well, yes," I admitted. "But only I wonder why you didn't keep it and give it to one of the men who has a dog team."

Both Eskimos shifted their positions to face me. We were all huddled comfortably inside sleeping bags. These had been laid on overturned skins of caribou, stretched face downwards to prevent the freshly moulting hair from entering our restricted atmosphere. A polar bear pelt covered the skins, trapping warm pockets of air between our bodies and the permafrost below.

"Out here, we do not take any chances," Mangitak began. "Maybe the dog was not as friendly as you think. What do we do if it bites us — even in play? There are no doctors or hospitals here. Maybe we would be injured. Maybe we would die because of it. We cannot take such chances."

He paused to see if I had understood. I had. No chances. It was the law of survival.

The following day we cut down again to the sea ice. It was surprisingly familiar, and even I found that I could recognize the silhouettes of ridges that we had passed on the way out. This was a significant revelation, kept discreetly to myself, because for the first time in all these days I at last felt competent to do something for myself. I knew that I could navigate us home, though I didn't expect to be called on to perform this vital service. The others hadn't considered me capable of doing anything so far.

On the sea ice, we met a party of hunters, heading in the direction from which we had just come. As we were still a hundred miles from Cape Dorset, they told us of the ice and snow conditions they had encountered. We, in turn, gave them information about the region where we had been.

Among the group was Saila Oshoochiak, Pitseolak's other brother, sometimes a carver, sometimes a government interpreter, but always the hunter. From the looks of their laden komatiks, I guessed that they planned to be away for a couple of weeks, though they seemed rather like a bunch of weekend fishermen trying to find a pub. But as my eyes ran along their barely visible faces, I recognized that the group was composed of some of the most expert hunters in this part of Baffin Island.

From the babble of words, I suddenly caught "amaro."

"What are they saying about wolves?" I asked Saila.

"Mangitak and Tytoosie are telling where it was that you got caribou. Ever since you killed these caribou, the wolves have been following your path. We wish to know exactly where you have been so that we can watch for them." He spoke with his usual quiet air. It was only a level above a whisper.

"Do what?" I erupted, far from quietly.

"Well, surely you realize that you've been followed by a pack of wolves for the last day or so." His manner was incredulous.

"Where are they now?" I asked to sidestep the question, scanning the apparent emptiness as I spoke. He looked around slowly, considering the direction we had come from and the cover the wolves would need to keep out of sight.

"I'd guess they're somewhere up there," he remarked casually. "Probably keeping a mile or so behind you." My amazement was ill-concealed apparently, for then he laughed and said, "My brother Mangitak tells me that they came outside the snow house you were sleeping in last night. They stole some meat from the komatik."

"Oh! I didn't know." I tried to sound matter-of-fact as I turned to look at the piles of meat on the sled.

Tytoosie gave the others some of the meat, and then we

parted company, heading off in different directions. Before long, it began to snow heavily, which didn't add to my comfort. I kept wondering how much nearer the wolves might come under the camouflage of the storm. I wasn't even sure how fast they could run. However, there was no sign of them when, after many hours, the snowstorm passed; under the clear blue mid-morning sky I could see nothing but the sparkling whiteness of newly fallen snow.

The loosely packed snow slowed us up a bit, so we paused for tea to allow it to freeze over. It was quite firm half an hour later when we were ready to make the final run into Cape Dorset. Soon, the upper ridge of Mallik Island came into view, then the high backbone of Cape Dorset Island. Finally, we turned the corner away from the floe edge and headed directly for home, the skidoo engines held flat out and komatiks zipping along behind them. The runners sliced over the snow, cutting with the precision of a scalpel and leaving an open gash peeling away behind us. I held on to my ropes tightly, feeling rather like a water-skier. It was exhilarating to watch the houses getting larger and larger, and then to see the scurrying, hooded ants become real people — Mary, Mosesee, Adamie, Kenojuak... all there, going about their everyday business.

Finally, we were back, stopping outside Oshoochiak's home, with the family coming out to see the size of the catch, to make sure that all was well and that there had been no mishaps. And then, before I had time to realize it, I was sitting in my own house, the kettle on for a drink, a package of soup being broken open, and Jill giving me a plate of bread and butter — "Just to keep you going until I can fix a proper meal."

It was odd that after being so closely tied together for almost a week, none of us had said farewell. Nor had I thanked Mangitak and Tytoosie. They had both gone off silently before I had the chance to do so. On the other hand, obviously we were all thankful that the catch had been a good one and that we were home safely. So why bother to express our thankfulness? It was another one of our southern pleasantries — another waste of time.

As I ate the plate of food and then enjoyed the pleasures of a long-awaited bath, I recalled how Pitseolak had once remarked to me that he no longer thought like an Eskimo. "How do Eskimos think?" I had asked. "I don't know," was his reply.

Freshly washed and dressed, I considered his remark. I had just spent many days watching two Eskimo hunters thinking, relentlessly using their initiative in order to survive. I knew that Pitseolak didn't think like that. Normally, no one does.

Nine

One Sunday, some weeks later, I had another illuminating experience — one that still remains most vivid. As on most Sundays, I had spent a considerable part of the afternoon gazing through the double-glazed window at the world outside. A blizzard was raging, casting snowflakes everywhere in a vicious haphazard manner. As the winds blew across the bay and smashed into the houses, they sent up smaller gusts over and around the buildings, whisking the snow with them. Much of the snow became firmly stuck to the sides of the walls, fastening there until the next gust slapped on successive layers. The only building that I could clearly discern was the one immediately in front of the window, and it too had now become almost entirely enveloped in white.

I rose from the armchair and went into the kitchen. Drafts swept along the floor, finding their way through cracks I had never dreamed existed. Away from the old black oven, my breath began to show itself as mist. I peeped through the kitchen window and looked at the thermometer, but a pocket of snowflakes had piled up in the corner of the pane, making it virtually impossible to see the thin red line of alcohol. Glancing beyond the thermometer, I could see that several large cartons of food supplies and an old tea chest, which I had placed out by the back door scarcely an hour before, had completely disappeared beneath a drift.

I returned to the innumerable scraps of paper that littered my desk — the fragments of a news report I was attempting to collate. But no sooner had I sat down than I heard a faint knock at the front door. It couldn't be Pitseolak, I knew that, even though he had recently come back from his training course. Pitseolak always burst in unceremoniously. As expected, I found a very different figure on the doorstep — six-year-old Mark. He was covered from head to foot in snow, his dog-fur trimming a blot of frozen moisture from his panting breath. He stood there in the cold, politely learning the way of the kadloonas and characteristically smiling.

"Can I come to visit?" he asked, making no effort to rush inside.

"Yes, of course, Mark. Quick, come in here, into the warm."

Mark had already removed his boots and parka by the time I had fastened the second door.

"How are you today?" I asked formally and traditionally.

"Fine, thank you," came the muffled reply from somewhere within his jettisoned clothing.

"It's very cold outside, Mark. Maybe you should be at home?"

"I wanted to come for a visit," he retorted, a grin flushing the full width of his tiny face. "I have a present for you." I glanced towards a grubby hand and watched while eager little fingers slowly unfurled. In the palm of his hand all that I could make out was a very crumpled piece of paper that looked as if it might once have been an envelope. Within, I spied a chequered piece of material.

"Thank you, Mark."

I had not the faintest idea what the offering might be.

In the middle of October, he had done the same thing. Then, however, his thoughtful gift had been a dead bird, produced from his pocket and wrapped in a piece of rag. The bird had been one that he had stoned himself. Like many other Eskimo children, he prided himself greatly at having succeeded in killing a bird with a small stone, though, in fact, most of them were much better shots than comparable youngsters elsewhere.

The mysterious package had now to be opened, and a half-dozen grotesque possibilities came to mind as I carefully unfurled it. The contents were a pleasant surprise. Deep in the fold of what I identified as having once been someone's shirt-tail was some desiccated coconut. Where on earth the boy could have acquired such an item I had no idea, indeed I never did find out.

"Oh, Mark!" I exclaimed, both in surprise and relief. "Thank you very much. It is very kind of you. Thank you!"

Before I could note his reaction he had run into the living room and was kneeling on the floor, playing with an empty spool from the typewriter. I had always admired the ability of the children to amuse themselves with what, for me, was absolutely nothing. Being born and raised in an area without shopping plazas, they had learned to use anything they could find. A cardboard box might become a hat, or a hiding place, or a shoe, or any one of a million other things which their inventive minds might deem feasible. I often watched them at play, changing the function and role of some domestic rubbish into innumerable games, playing for hours on end with absorbed delight. Mark had decided that the spool was a skidoo and he was sliding it merrily across the carpet.

When Jill joined us, she was as intrigued by the coconut as I had been.

"Mark, it's lovely!" she said, pointing to the rag. "Where did you get it?"

"My mother," he snapped back, as if objecting to the intrusion which the words were having on his skidoo ride.

"Does your mother know you are here?" It did, after all, seem highly irregular that a little boy barely beyond infancy should have made his way across the snowdrifts in a fearful blizzard. There were many other houses he could have visited much closer to home. He chose to ignore the question. As his own house did not have a telephone, I couldn't even call his parents to let them know where he was.

"I want a drink," he demanded suddenly.

"Pardon? What do you say?" My response was instinctive.

"I want a drink, *pleeez*."

This whole question of courtesy was a minor source of irritation to all concerned, for the Eskimo language is fundamentally devoid of such pleasantries. Living in the tundra, everything operates on the same level. There is no superficiality, no acting, no changing behaviour from day to day or from person to person.

Unlucky hunters see it as their right to share in the successes of another, and they simply take a portion of meat without asking. To deny food could be to deny life to someone upon whom you might in turn have to depend. I had once sat in a house and watched a man enter, remove a rifle, and depart without even as much as a friendly hello.

"He knows I don't need it today, otherwise I would already be out hunting with it instead of carving," clarified my companion when he noted my raised eyebrows.

"When will he bring it back?" I had asked. Not a single syllable had been uttered during the borrowing.

"I don't know," he remarked casually. "But if I need one tomorrow, then I'll go and take someone else's."

It had, for me, summed it all up. And Mark, knowing full well that we had a drink in the house, had not entertained the notion that it would be denied him. But he said "pleeez" nevertheless — it was the way of the kadloonas.

"Was it good?" I asked as he ended the noisy guzzling. Another superfluous question, I noted to myself. So much of our conversation is unnecessary. How economical with words are the Eskimos!

"Yes," Mark said, going into the kitchen. I heard him wash the cup and then detected his stockinged feet padding their way into the bathroom.

Before long, the tap was gushing furiously. Clearly, he had decided to take a full-scale strip-down wash. Splashing sounds could be heard from the room. Then came the inevitable squelching noise of soapy bubbles being forced through Mark's fingers. It was all quite usual, for our bathroom was more than adequately equipped, and the majority of our visitors took the opportunity to spread water over themselves, the walls, and floors. But the bathroom was always tidied and made neat and clean before they departed, for this too was part of the ablution ritual.

It seemed a contradiction to me, that after the government had gone to the costly trouble of providing the families of the settlement with comfortable prefabricated homes, complete with sink unit and often a bathtub, very few were supplied with running water. Whereas I could turn on taps and receive either hot or cold water on demand, these facilities had seldom been connected in Eskimo houses. Pitseolak frequently lamented how he still had to go outside with a saucepan for snow and then melt it over the hot plate; or chip a piece of ice from the family's supply and then melt that over the heat.

"Cramps my style," he had once remarked. "Just think how many saucepans it takes for me to have a bath!"

I jerked away from these thoughts. There was now a sound coming from the bathroom that was neither bubble-bursting nor splashing. Aghast, we both realized what it might be. Jill was the first to arrive on the scene. There, behind the shower curtain on hands and knees was Mark squirting toothpaste over the tiles. An avant-garde piece of bas-relief distorted itself as it ran and trickled through the edges and joins. At the same time, Mark was cleaning his teeth furiously — with my brush. He looked up, face covered in green fluoride, and successfully dissolved my displeasure with a flash of that award-winning smile. As he glowed, he stuck the end of the brush into his ear, removed some of the wax, and then enthusiastically reverted to the task in hand. Words defied me, and I departed as Mark said brightly, "Me washing these!" — indicating his front teeth.

Mark tidied up after himself. He took great pains to wash and clean the mirror — with my face cloth — and was soon once more on the floor playing with the spool, which had now become a spinning top. Outside the blizzard continued to howl.

The playing, washing, and drinking had occupied the best part of an hour, and both Jill and I agreed that it was high time Mark went home — his parents might be worrying — and we felt that the least we could do was to take him back to his father's house. Mark's father was Peter Pitseolak, the noted carver and painter whose work is featured in so many books and galleries across Canada. He lived at the bottom of an incline, in that sort of position that real estate agents tend to describe as a "lakeside home with great potential." Around the property, Peter Pitseolak had erected a low fence, so that the first impression was that the house itself might have been a trailer, permanently resting in some authorized campsite.

Without knocking, the three of us burst into the living room. Like the use of "Please" and "Thank you," this whole business of knocking is dispensed with as an unnecessary pleasantry. Nobody — except polite little

Mark — would dream of standing outside in a howling blizzard, waiting perhaps several minutes for the occupant to get to the door.

We found Peter Pitseolak seated at the table, drawing with an assorted array of felt pens. The house was quiet and calm as he steadily placed well-contemplated lines and curves onto the white paper. A strange bird formed itself there, its elongated neck rising heavenward with soft arabesques in which a laughing figure hovered apprehensively.

After a while Peter looked up, smiled at us, and then growled some words to his son. He seemed to be reprimanding the boy for venturing into the storm and disturbing our household. I tried to explain that Mark had caused us no inconvenience — though this wasn't as easy as might be imagined, since my ability to speak Eskimo was on a par with Peter's English.

"Mark very good. Me very happy. Mark in my house. Everybody very happy." I ploughed on in basic Eskimo, accompanying my words with explanatory gestures, arms flamboyantly flapping this way and that, fingers exaggeratedly pointing at myself, at Jill, at Mark — and then out of the window to indicate "snow" and "bad weather."

"Koviakshookpunga," I concluded — and then realized that, due to my mispronunciation, I had said something closer to "Merry Christmas" than "I am happy." For a moment there was silence in the room. Then Peter laughed and returned to his work. And his wife, who had been lingering in the background, came forward with cups of tea.

During the next quarter of an hour, Jill and I stretched our limited vocabulary to the utmost as we drank our tea and tried to converse with our hosts. Peter grunted and threw in the odd word, without needing to abandon his bird. I was feeling that it was about time we left when, looking out of the steamy window, I saw two hooded shapes approaching the house: Paouta and Sapah. Paouta was now an aging man, but ten years earlier he had been heralded as one of the greatest carvers in the entire Canadian Arctic. I had seen examples of his work long before I came north, the most notable being a huge piece of carved stone that I had come across in a park in Toronto. Made for an outdoor art exhibition many years earlier, it had squatted there casually, slightly eroded by the elements, scarred by the declarations of young lovers, and obviously used regularly by an ignorant dog population. It had struck me then that this unrevered lump of stone was by far the most valuable exhibit in the park — doubtless worth thousands of dollars.

Sapah was much younger than Paouta — in his early twenties — and he spoke good English as well as fluent French. He had been born in Arctic Quebec and had gone to school there, later becoming an assistant at the school. But after a couple of years he had migrated to Baffin Island with his family. His father, Simon Aliqu, was a talented carver who had hoped that there might be a more consistent outlet for his work in Cape Dorset than there was in Quebec.

I told Sapah about Mark and the coconut, and asked him to explain the whole thing to the child's parents. Obligingly, he did so, but no sooner had he finished speaking than Mark's mother let fly with what sounded like an emotional outburst. Then Peter joined in, then Paouta. Listening to the torrent without being able to understand a word, I could only presume that something had gone very wrong.

"Are they annoyed, or what?" I asked Sapah nervously.

"Oh no. Not at all. They are very happy that Mark was out to visit you, and they are equally pleased that you have come to visit them. They hope Mark did not annoy you, and they say that if he was not well behaved they will have words with him."

"But what else did they say?" They had been talking for about fifteen minutes.

"Oh, they got to discussing the hunting trip Paouta is hoping to make and the picture Peter is drawing and a child in the nursing station who has some kind of flu."

Mark, I noticed, was putting on his boots and parka. Without a word of farewell or explanation, he slipped quietly away to make another visit. Nobody called him back. The wind was still very forceful, coming from the northeast, whisking down the slopes of Mallik Island and then tearing towards us across the flat five miles of sea ice. As I watched Mark trudge off, his head well down, I saw a larger figure emerge out of the storm. The human bundle blew in through the door. It was Pitseolak.

"What's a fine fellow like you doing out on a day like this?" I asked as he lowered his hood and rubbed his hands vigorously.

He grinned. "Nothing wrong with the weather." Then he slid down onto the floor and lay there full-length, his head propped against the wall. He too was given a cup of tea.

As I chatted to Pitseolak, I realized that here was an opportunity not to be missed. There were all sorts of questions that I had long been storing in my mind, and this was the moment to ask them — while I was in the company of the two elders together with two interpreters. Through Pitseolak and Sapah I asked a few general questions, just to make sure that my curiosity would not be resented. Obviously it would not be: Paouta and Peter reacted enthusiastically to my interest. So I moved on to more specific areas.

"Pitseolak," I said, "last summer I made a long journey on foot to the other side of Cape Dorset Island, and after

about four hours we came across an old abandoned campsite. Could you ask them if they know anything about the
place — how old it is, what it's called, and so on?''

Pitseolak was intrigued and set about the task eagerly.
As they chatted, I could again clearly form pictures of that
curious place. When I had been there, I had felt something
strange about the site: an invisible, imperceptible aura
suggesting death and mysticism. There had been an
eeriness about the silence that smothered what had once
been a bustling centre. However, I had been unable to learn
anything about the place. Although most people in Cape
Dorset seemed to have heard of the spot, no one had been
able to give me its name, for example, or even tell me about
the original inhabitants. Maybe I was wrong. Perhaps no
one did know anything.

"How did you get there?" Peter asked. "Did you come
along the valley?"

I explained that we had reached the site by following
the great glacial valleys that are etched diagonally across
Cape Dorset Island. We had become slightly lost — for we
were merely following a scanty verbal description which
someone had given us that same morning — and had
eventually climbed too high up the slopes of the biggest
valley.

"I first saw the camp from high up on one of the hills
that overlooks the site," I said. "We were looking down
towards a shallow bay, with a small sandy beach with rocks
jutting out on either side. The campsite was up a level or so
from the beach, on a flat patch of grass."

As my words were translated, both men stared intently,
nodding simultaneously that they knew precisely what I
was referring to. I then mentioned some cairns which we
had encountered during the course of the descent. Doubtless, they would have been visible from below, for they
seemed to pierce the route — I had physically brushed by

them — and they intrigued me probably more than the many other things that were there. I longed to know exactly what they were and why they had been built, for I sensed that they hovered over the former cluster of dwellings like centurions guarding a defenseless city; they had power both in firmness of construction and also by location. I was also curious to know whether any of this heritage was still lingering in the back of these old men's minds.

"The view from the top was very beautiful," I continued. "And, from what I could gather, the location of the campsite had been very wisely selected by these distant peoples. It was angled against the apparent prevailing wind, close to the water and yet raised high above the waterline. Pitseolak, ask them if they know what the cairns were used for."

The resulting conversation was lengthy and complex, the words spoken slowly and deliberately. Every so often Paouta would interject, offer a contribution, and retire again thoughtfully. Once or twice, Peter and Paouta went into a huddle all of their own so that neither of the younger men could distinctly follow their deliberations; they seemed to be cross-checking facts with one another.

At last Pitseolak translated: "They say the men of that campsite used to go hunting for polar bear and walrus which lived across the waters on Southampton Island. The hunters would often be gone for a long time, and they had to travel a long way in their kayaks. They say that these were the men who built the cairns you have seen. They used them so that they could see where they were, so that when they got back to the coast of Baffin Island they could look for their own cairns and know where to make for."

"Did these cairns have any other significance for the men, other than simply being markers to tell them where they were?"

Sapah asked my question and the men laughed.

"They said they had meaning because when the hunters saw them they knew they were home again — and could be with their wives in bed again, instead of being alone in their kayaks!"

Everyone was laughing, we all were. But I was still not really content with the answers. When I had first broached the topic, some telltale movements of the eyes, or the pursing of a lip, had indicated that some significance was associated with the rock piles greater than any of this.

"Was there anything in them?" I pursued. The mirth ended immediately.

"They want to know what you mean," said Pitseolak.

"How were the cairns built? Just like a pile of stones? Ask them why these hunters did not build something like an inookshook, like they do along the tracks used for the caribou. Something like that would have been much taller and far easier to see."

My question was relayed across the room, from one ear to the next, and the reply came back via an equally circuitous route: "They say that the cairns are just piles of stones. The men did not build inookshooks because they wanted to make their markers like that. They could have built inookshooks but they do not know why they built one thing and not the other. This was all a very long time ago."

I indicated acceptance, nodded and smiled. Then, as a casual aside to Pitseolak, I commented that I regretted not having taken a closer look: "There might have been something inside or around the base of them. I might have found something."

My remark was passed automatically along the line, and I was surprised at the look of horror on the elders' faces.

"No! You shouldn't do that!" snapped back their reaction.

"I, too, am starting to think that these cairns of yours are maybe something more important," said Sapah.

"Well, ask them," I prodded. He did.

"It is quite true that the hunters used them as markers," began Peter, "and that they used them to guide them back to safety — although it is also clear that they could have used the profile of the hills to do this just as effectively. We still use such natural shapes to help us when we are out hunting today." Paouta bowed agreement as the translation was made.

Then Peter continued: "Before going on one of their hunting trips for polar bears, the hunters would approach the cairns and place something from their own person inside them. This might have been a necklace, an article of clothing, or really anything readily associated with that particular hunter. When the hunter came back, he would retrieve it. The cairns were their symbol of safety."

"Did they say anything at the cairn before departing? As if it was an altar?"

"No, we do not think that they did this, but we do not know. I believe only that the cairns were symbols to these men, their hopes for a good hunt and their targets for a safe return. Perhaps they were symbols of safety. We do not believe that they worshipped them. Or that they were gods."

As this in turn was relayed to me, Peter faltered, as if to gather his thoughts a little more clearly. He screwed up his old wrinkled face, ground his teeth, and then stroked his nose. He was a religious man and this was important.

"I think," he continued, "that we can say that the cairns were, in fact, a focal point of their faith, both for those departing as well as for those who had to wait anxiously for the hunters to return. The cairns must have gone with the men as clear images — like vivid pictures in their minds — knowing that their families would be looking at the same cairns and, in a way, praying to them for a safe trip. It could be that this was a part of their informal religion."

I asked what Peter felt about this sort of thing as an elder of the local Anglican mission. He replied that he did not believe in idols and in many gods, as had the people of his past. At the same time, he was eager to urge that those beliefs should not be belittled or ridiculed.

"Let's just say," he grinned, "that although I have been to the campsite of which you talk, I have never been anywhere near these cairns. I would not touch them!"

Added Paouta: "After all, this is what they believed in, and if it helped them to get back safely, gave them something to have faith in, then it couldn't have been bad." I couldn't help but agree with his philosophical wisdom.

Peter, meanwhile, was pointing his bony finger towards a small dresser. His wife rose and started to look through a pile of papers, and when she couldn't find whatever it was, Peter himself started rummaging, methodically ploughing through shoe boxes and scraps of paper. After a while, he tossed a rather tattered jewellery box onto the table.

"What's he got in there?" I asked Pitseolak.

"I'm not sure, but I think that they have something they want to show you. It's something for you to look at — possibly some notes or pictures. I'm not sure."

"Peter's photographs," explained Paouta.

For the next hour and a half we sat poring over an astounding array of memorabilia — a disorganized and haphazard collection of pictures which revealed the historical evolution of Cape Dorset during the vital last twenty-five years. Another box was spirited from beneath the bed, a dilapidated shoe box. From the remnants of a label on one end, I could see that long ago it had held a pair of expensive suede shoes. Peter picked his way carefully through the disjointed layers of photographs, Paouta arching his body so that he could snatch a brief preview of each photo before the rest of us. This collection was even more intriguing, revealing people and places so radically altered that the older men frequently paused for lengthy periods before announcing names, identities, places, and locations.

"This is the Hudson's Bay store, long before the other buildings were added out back."

"Do you know who that is? It's Matthewsee's father!"

"This is me with my first wife."

"Most attractive!"

"Yes, most."

"I'm not sure who that is — maybe Inookee's father and some other people who lived out at camp."

"I think that this lady here is Etushakjuak as a girl," Peter said to Pitseolak, with clear reference to the youth's dead natural mother. We looked through partially squinting eyes, but the entire picture was out of focus and the face at the back of the group was reduced to a sepia blur. She must have moved.

Suddenly, I caught a glimpse of the hands of Peter's watch. It was already late, and I still had to complete my newscast and then record it before the scheduled plane arrived from Frobisher in the morning.

"Tell me if you see anything outstanding," I called to Pitseolak from the doorway. And then added as a frustrated afterthought, "In fact, tell me about them all tomorrow."

He waved acknowledgement without bothering to turn. He was totally immersed in these stacks of pictures which represented his hidden past. For me the photographs were like some fabled voyage into a different and fascinating world that I had previously only been able to imagine. But, for Pitseolak, it was part of a more urgent quest for identity.

If now I care to take a step back into that room, I can clearly see the shapes huddled protectively over photographs and boxes — chatter and laughter interspersed with spells of silence. But, within this, I am always left more vividly with the picture of just two of those who sat there that day: Peter Pitseolak, tired and aging, reliving his youth in what would be the last year of his life. Then, in his shadow, sits the vibrant excited shape of a much younger man — uselessly learning, unaware of the bleak future that awaited him. The unfinished drawing of the bird sits behind them.

Ten

Visibility was negligible the day I went to the airstrip to see Pitseolak off to Alert, where he was to start the full mechanic's course. Not even the local postmaster was expecting the plane to leave Frobisher Bay, let alone land amidst the swirling snows of Cape Dorset shortly after noon. So convinced was he that nothing was due that he was out the back somewhere in a shack, repairing his prized Mustang snowmobile when he heard the first dronings overhead. The plane made a couple of flyovers, the second lower than the first, and then nestled cautiously onto the sea ice.

The scene was then all action. The engines of the ancient DC 3 didn't stop spinning the propellors for fear that they might freeze up; the blades turned idly in the misty air. Wooden blocks were positioned fore and aft of the huge rubber wheels, and wedges were forced beneath the skis upon which they rested. Inevitably, it would be a relatively long stop — not the quick in-and-out type of trip which the crew would have preferred in these poor weather conditions — for the Co-op needed to ship southwards stacks of crates containing valuable soapstone carvings.

Technically, the plane was on charter from Nordair by the West Baffin Eskimo Co-operative; but, as usual, there were people who needed to clamber aboard and fill the few seats that hadn't been removed to accommodate the priceless cargo. Two of these seats had been reserved by DNA for Eteloo and Pitseolak.

"Well, this looks like it," I said not too imaginatively to Eteloo, waving an arm towards the blur that stood scarcely thirty yards from where we were standing. Panepak, bandy-legged from the weight of a particularly heavy box, dragged himself to the doorway and heaved it up to a crew member. Snow flurries had already blown through the hatch, depositing a delicate layer of white down across the flooring.

"Yes, this is it. I'm off," Eteloo replied. "I hope the weather is better than this in Frobisher."

"You should worry! If you're worried about this, then just think what's probably going on up in Alert this very same moment. You'll be longing for anything this mild in a few weeks."

"Can't bear to think about it!" He shrugged, blinding his eyes with a mitten. But, in fact, Eteloo was about to do what he wanted to do most of all, and he knew that one day he would become an expert in settlement engineering.

"Wonder where Pitseolak is?" I said.

We both turned towards the vague outline of houses. Skidoos were still weaving over the ice in our direction. People continued to approach the plane, and a hastily loaded sled was bounding its way towards us, bright blue mail bags precariously balanced along its entire length. Amidst a white spray, the postmaster came in pursuit, rapidly gaining speed as he thundered forward with the impact of a finely tuned snowplough.

"Can't see him," I said.

"He's probably still looking for the rest of his silk ties," chuckled a voice nearby.

We turned and saw the giant shape of Munarmee-kudluk, his gangling frame draped against the side of his bombardier as if he was some spectator at a Sunday junior league soccer match. Munarmeekudluk was outrageously tall for an Eskimo, or any other ethnic group for that matter, and he sported a scrupulously groomed goatee which was equally unusual in this land of bristeless men. He was about twenty-eight years old, one of those vital people that every community in the world has — or should have — who is loved by all as a necessary escape from reality. Totally reliable in helping anyone at all, he was always ready to give a toothy laugh when it was needed most.

I had long called him Mr. Munarmeekudluk. Somehow, he had a bearing, a manner which seemed to warrant this bonus of titled respect. I suppose that it also set him apart from everyone else — not that he wasn't out on a different tangent anyway. His English was excellent, spoken flawlessly — if one could ignore the curious accent of northern England which occasionally surfaced when least expected. "Quyte nyce, loov," he would compliment. The truth of this linguistic peculiarity was that he had once fallen madly in love with a teacher and had been invited all the way back to Bradford, England, to meet her parents. "Foony playce, that," he would sometimes reflect.

He was thus a world traveller, one who could speak casually of shopping in Woolworth's and sitting in the back row of the Regal Cinema on a Saturday night. He'd seen it all, jumped typically feet first from life in Cape Dorset into that of suburban Bradford. I had often wondered what the girl's parents had thought of the strange ways of Mr. Munarmeekudluk and what the girl herself would have used as a surname had they ever married — for he didn't have one of his own.

Mr. Munarmeekudluk was certainly a "character." He always wore a corduroy, Tyrolean-type bonnet ("Got it in Marks 'n Sparks for three and six," he once confided to me.) He had been one of those singled out by nature to start balding early, and by the age of twenty-three his hair had receded as two parallel bays from above each eyebrow — then abruptly halted midway to the crown. Between these shining patches, a tuft of hair some two inches wide stood high to the winds, proud of its survival. However, it was rarely seen because of the all-concealing protection of the corduroy hat.

"What are you doing here?" I asked. "Not off on a trip?"

"No, I'm looking after the bombardier for DNA," he replied. "They told me to keep an eye on it for them, so I thought that I'd come out and watch the others working." He slapped his thigh and guffawed generously with deep breaths that resembled those of a neighing horse. We laughed infectiously — at him, rather than at his remark.

"No, but seriously," he said, "seriously though folks, Pitseolak will be along any minute now." Then he added, "As soon as he finds his satin waistcoat!" Once more he was laughing.

Munarmeekudluk liked a good laugh and responded with particular enthusiasm to his own jokes. And when he laughed, his legs jellied into a modified Charleston and he clapped his enormous hands as if they were two crashing cymbals. When in full swing, with his gangling frame unable to guarantee further balance, he would zig-zag in reverse to the nearest wall in the hope of being able to remain erect with its support. No doubt, that was why he was now leaning against the yellow sides of the snowcat.

Pitseolak was still nowhere to be seen, and it crossed my mind that perhaps he had got the days mixed up. But then I realized that this couldn't be so, for everyone had been talking about the departure of these two sons for weeks now. It was inconceivable that Pitseolak didn't know that this was the plane he was to go on.

"Wonder where he's got to," remarked Eteloo.

"I still don't see him," I replied anxiously.

"Foony lad, that," came the voice from behind. "Right foony lad."

It was the absence of an outburst of laughter that caused me to turn towards the battered vehicle. Munarmeekudluk was sprawled against the side, his feet poking narrow trenches into the snow. Random lines etched with the side of his foot, as if he was doodling.

"Why so serious, lad?" I asked.

"Just thinking. You know, I had all these chances some years back. They wanted me to train for this and learn that. As you know, I've even been to England, so I've seen a lot of things and have been to a lot of places. I have some pretty good ideas as to what it's all about and what's going on in that big world outside of here." He stretched his arms to their full towering height above his head and let out a lengthy yawn.

"Then, one day, when I was out with a neat little string bag shopping in Bradford High Street for sausages, or something like that, I got to wondering. I could have stayed in England, you know. Married and got a nice respectable job. I'd have had a family, a car, paid my bills and income tax just like all the others." He was staring blankly at nothing, his mind transported to the neat rows of houses with matching brick walls and carefully tended gardens. The flowers would be starting to blossom: roses, forget-me-nots, dahlias. The lawn would need cutting, and the edges of the flower beds would have to be trimmed and plucked of weeds.

"But that day," he continued, "when we were out shopping, getting eggs, bread, and milk, and all those things, I got to thinking that really I belonged back here. And I realized that that lass wouldn't have been happy to live here all her life, just as I knew that her world of ties and polished shoes wasn't for me. I knew what I truly wanted more than anything was to be back here, right here, in Cape Dorset."

115

He heaved a foot at the powdery snow and sent a cloud up around our knees; not viciously, but more out of the purpose of emphasizing "right here."

"This is my home," he said firmly. "I belong here. I'm an Eskimo. I decided that I didn't want to spend the rest of my life pretending I was someone else. So that's why I'm here. No big mystery. So I came back, married my wife. I have my children and I'm a hunter. Free and contented. I'm an Eskimo."

All this had been somewhat unexpected, and we had temporarily forgotten that Eteloo was about to embark on a new career.

"Of course, that's just how I feel, that's me," added Mr. Munarmeekudluk, in an obvious attempt to downgrade what he had been saying. "Seen Pitseolak?" he shouted to a figure who had just arrived on a skidoo. Then he turned to me and blurted, "He'd better forget about his dancing shoes and hightail it over here if he wants to catch the plane." Laughing once more, he duly careened backwards into the metal side of the bombardier.

I peered at the aircraft. Its engines were now starting to rev slightly in preliminary test to check that ice hadn't formed on the inside. The increased noise indicated that all was still well, but the change of pitch jostled the carriers and packers into greater activity, and a handful of passengers began to clamber aboard.

"I'd better get on it," said Eteloo. His emotions were visibly mixed between excitement and happiness, but tainted by the natural sorrow of leaving home for a long, long time.

We shook hands and said the usual farewells. We would probably never meet again. Then he spoke briefly with his father — I hadn't even noticed him standing some distance to our right — and he went to the side door. Without proper metal steps, which would have sunk into the accumulating depth of snow, he vaulted onto the cold floor of the plane. Someone tossed his bag up, he smiled, waved and disappeared among the shadows inside.

"Where on earth is Pitseolak?" I repeated. I began to wonder if he was sick. It was odd that not one member of his family was here.

In the small, curious crowd that now hovered near the hatchway, I caught sight of George, the senior DNA administrator, the man who had set Pitseolak on the path to Alert. His eyes were darting anxiously beneath his bushy white eyebrows. Obviously, he too was wondering what on earth had happened.

I looked back towards the settlement, hoping to see Pitseolak come tearing across the whiteness on the back of a skidoo, baggage a-flying, arms waving wildly. But there was nothing. Only a few stragglers making their way home. Eteloo was peering through a side window of the aircraft, and we shrugged shoulders at each other and raised our hands in despair. George took one last look round and then slammed the door and sealed it tight with a wrenching twist of the lever.

After the plane had gone, Munarmeekudluk gave me a lift back to the settlement. As we bounced across the brittle ice, I realized that this was the first time we had ever had such a deeply serious conversation. Underneath his geniality, he too had faced the cultural conflict, the same conflict that troubled Pitseolak. It was an impossibly difficult conflict, I realized. We, the good Samaritans, were offering the Inuit a very dubious alternative — a dilemma.

Munarmeekudluk was all joviality, forever the court jester, as we bounced over the ice. There were more jokes about Pitseolak's waistcoat, but I found it hard to produce suitably witty replies. Where was Pitseolak? What had happened? Why hadn't he boarded the plane?

It was almost a week before I learned the answer.

Eleven

From the polite tapping, I could tell that someone was already inside. Outside, and therefore beyond the layers of insulation which cocooned the house, it would have been a much more muffled sound, as if someone was flicking a cardboard box.

I was in the bathroom for the weekly trimming of my beard, and as I hurried to see who it was, I was still rubbing my face to dislodge the odd severed bristle.

"Oh, it's you, Pitseolak," I said through the towelling. This was the first time I had seen him since his non-appearance at the airport, but I decided to underreact. "Come in and take a seat. Won't be a minute. I'm just finishing a quick shaving job."

I made to go back into the bathroom but suddenly noticed out of the corner of my eye that Pitseolak's hand was outstretched towards the inner doorway. He had someone with him.

"This is my cousin," he said, motioning towards the half light by the coat hangers.

I saw nothing and so advanced some more paces, lowered the towel with one hand, and peered towards the corner. Akeeagok* came out to greet me.

*Author's note: I have substituted this pseudonym instead of his real name.

"He speaks no English and is a hunter," offered Pitseolak.

We shook hands. Akeeagok had a warm but wild air about him. I thought at the time that he reminded me of an Indian scout in some Western, the one who had just returned to the cavalry fort after being out on the trail for a few weeks. He laughed with his eyes and grinned broadly. His face was the dirty-ochre colouring which is the trademark of those who have been overexposed to the winds, snows, and sunburns of the tundra. His hair was black, dishevelled, combed with fingers. He was a little taller than either of us, and it was obvious that beneath his well-worn clothing he had a very powerful and muscular frame. He released his hold on my hand, and I could still feel the grip lingering for some time afterwards.

"Come in, Akeeagok," I said through gestures. His trousers were greasy, and above one knee I noticed a shiny patch, as if a knife blade had habitually been wiped clean in the same place for many years. His kamiks had lost most of their silvery seal hair and were threadbare through continual use. I had seen him before, infrequently. Akeeagok was a hunter, a man of the land, uncomfortable with the unfamiliar.

"...didn't even go to school," Pitseolak was saying, "spent most of his time out hunting with his father."

I smiled. There was something in Pitseolak's tone that was different, something intangible which I had detected even as he had first said hello to me some minutes earlier. I realized that he was not trying to apologize for his friend's lack of formal education, nor was he really warning me that I might have a slight communication problem. I felt that he spoke with pride — was showing me a *real* Eskimo, someone unadulterated by cultural intrusion.

Also, for the first time I now actually noticed Pitseolak's appearance. He was totally changed, totally altered from the suave young man that I had so often entertained. He looked as if he had just got up. His hair was unkempt, and I noticed that those strands which were normally greased into an immaculate quiff had been inexpertly trimmed to nothing. I also failed to catch those smells of the well-groomed young man-about-town. No Eau de Cologne — he hadn't even shaved. His windbreaker was scuffed, and he didn't seem to care.

Since I hadn't even seen Pitseolak since that day when he had failed to get on the plane with Eteloo, I had not had a chance to talk to him. He had almost gone underground, out of circulation.

"Hey, what happened to Alert?" I casually asked. "The plane's long since gone — plus one empty seat! How come you missed it?"

His eyes sparkled, he grinned and shrugged his shoulders. Just like the old Pitseolak again. "Changed my mind," he declared with a cheeky smile.

"But I thought it was all sewn up. I thought that that was to be your chosen career. Your future. You even went out to Frobisher for that course. You told me you were dead keen on the whole idea."

He laughed briefly and cocked his head. "Just changed my mind, that's all. I'm not going."

I took a deep breath and sighed, but tried to keep in tune with the thinly veiled humour of the situation. "You're something else!" I exclaimed. I shook my head to and fro several times.

Akeeagok smiled. He hadn't the slightest idea what we were talking about. We could have been discussing hula-hula girls or interplanetary rocket ships for all he knew.

"I have things I want to talk to you about," Pitseolak said quietly. I knew from his sincerity that these were to be serious things, things he wanted me to understand with all his heart. I said nothing, didn't move, but waited for him to speak.

He rubbed his hands, picked at a dirty fingernail, and

jerked his head so that his eyes abruptly fastened to mine.

"I think of you as my friend," he began. "We have talked a great deal and you know me well." I fixed my sight onto the wall light, but he knew that I was listening to every word. "I have talked to you of my troubles and you have spoken to me like a brother. For this I am very grateful. You have always had time to talk with me, Jill too, and you have helped me in many ways."

My forehead nestled into the palm of my hand, and I closed my eyes. Pitseolak was looking down at the carpet. Akeeagok gazed tenderly and soberly at his cousin. He knew that it was serious talking now.

"You have always told me that it is my own life," continued Pitseolak, "and that I must make all the final decisions. That no one must do this for me. That I must do what I want to do. That I must decide because it is my life." His outstretched hands touched thoughtfully, fingertip to fingertip. He looked directly at me. "You have told me this often?"

I nodded gently.

"Well, I have thought about it a lot." He breathed heavily and deeply into the emotional silence. "I have thought about it carefully, and now I want to tell you about Alert — about everything." He was looking down again.

"When I first came to visit you, I came because I knew that you were Mangitak's friend. He and others told me about you and your wife, and I wanted to visit you. I also came, I guess, because I wanted to speak in English. Maybe to show you how good I was! In my house, I cannot speak in English to anyone like I have been speaking with you two in your house. But I think that maybe I just wanted to sit once more in a comfortable armchair, like this, with my feet on a carpet, to look at neatly framed pictures on the walls, to hear the radio, and read newspapers and magazines. I wanted to drink tea and coffee from a cup with a saucer, and I liked the sugar bowl on the table, biscuits on a plate, and a milk jug on the tray. I liked all of these things. I missed them. In my father's house we drink from those metal mugs and we shake sugar from a bag and stir with anything that is handy.

"I liked all the things here. Meals at the table. Knives and forks. Custard and fruit for dessert. Always something different to eat. Soup. I felt at home here, happy, and sometimes I even wished that I could sleep here, stay in a bedroom all for myself, with white sheets and blankets, and carpets on the floor. In my father's house, I share a room with Audla. It's so small. I have nowhere to put my things, no bookshelf, no neat little cupboard for my own things. Audla has pictures from magazines stuck on the wall — I don't even like them. Others use my shaving kit. Nothing is truly mine! There are too many people always everywhere. Lots of noise. I cannot go anywhere for peace and quiet. Your papers I found torn up and on the floor — but I don't know who did it, or why. You see, I have nowhere that is really my own. All of these things I could find here in your house, with you and Jill. Maybe I envied them and wanted just to stay here and be with you, right here.

"Then we talked about my life and what I would do. You were right when you told me that I would have to do something, that I couldn't go on doing nothing for ever, that I couldn't just keep taking money from my father. And I knew that I must think about my life and the years ahead. I thought of becoming a school assistant, even of going away again and becoming a teacher, then returning here to work, right in this schoolhouse over there. When I talked with DNA, I thought of working in the office, of typing letters, reports, and sitting all day at a desk with filing cabinets in the room. I thought, too, of the money I would make and of the things I would buy — clothes, records, new things for the house, a clock, an electric razor for myself. I'd buy a carpet for our room and some nice chairs. I could see all these things. It would be a new world for all of us, for me, my family, and our home. Everything would be different, and I could be right here working in Cape Dorset with my own room at DNA, my own office, desk and chair."

Pitseolak nestled back into the cushions as if he was deliberately trying to disturb the dream of what might have been, but now wouldn't happen.

"When they said I could become a mechanic, I was also pleased. I would learn something new and be better than all of the others. I wanted to be the first Eskimo completely in charge of the generators and all things here in Cape Dorset. And I knew that I could do it. When I went to Frobisher to learn all about it, I was happy at first. They explained how to fix and repair things, and I drove the heavy equipment and understood it, how it worked. I knew that I would be good at it. Even when they suggested that Eteloo and I should go to Alert, I was very happy. We would make good money. I thought that I might even stay up there longer than just six months, perhaps a year or even two. I could learn everything at Alert and then come back here and be in charge of everything, the heavy equipment too.

"Then, one day, I asked the man when I would be able to come back home to Cape Dorset and be in charge. It was then that I realized I was dreaming about the far-distant future. He told me that I'd have to wait for a vacancy here, but that there were always jobs in other settlements for Eskimos. Maybe I'd go to Pond Inlet or to Igloolik to work. He told me perhaps I could not come and get a job here for many years, maybe never.

"All of this made me think. You see, I was surprised. They seemed to be training me for something that would make me be away from my family again. I didn't want that. I'd been away from everybody too long already. I wanted to stay with them for always. That is the way it is with

Eskimos — we like to be together with our families and not scattered about here and there like the kadloonas. It seemed as if we had always been apart, and now that we were all together again, I wanted us never to break up. Mangitak, Audla, Martha, Saila, my father — everybody — we were all together again. I even spoke with my sister Kupa in Frobisher, and so I knew that she would soon be coming back home with her new baby. I just didn't want to leave everybody.

"So I started to think about all these things over again, about going away, about Alert. I knew, too, because this man had told me, that if I went away I might never come back to live with my family again. One night, I went to the movies in Frobisher and when I came out I met some Eskimo boys I knew, and we went to their house to drink. And we drank and drank, and I got drunk. Someone said something about my sister and it made me angry and we had a fight. But when we woke in the morning, we were not drunk and we were friends again. So we spoke about how bad liquor is and what it does, but my friends laughed. They said they didn't care, that they liked it."

Pitseolak looked straight at me. "That's what they're like in Frobisher. They're different Eskimos, not like us here. With their buses, shops, hard hats, fancy boots, overalls, jobs, and lots of money to spend. They're not like Eskimos at all!" Bitterly he dismissed the transcultural oddities, as he saw them.

"Anyway, I was still thinking about myself and what would happen to me. I knew that I didn't want to be like them, that I wanted to stay with my family and friends here. I didn't want to go away, anywhere. I didn't want to gamble my money away at card games in Alert. I wanted to be with my own people. And I knew that I would be happier, even if I had no job and no money and nothing to do but walk around and waste my time. So, when I got back from

Frobisher, I knew that I would not go on the plane with Eteloo, that he would have to go on his own — because he wanted to go there anyway. When the plane came, I stayed in my father's house and said that I was not going to go away but that I wanted to stay here with my family. When the plane took off, I was happy, even though my father didn't really understand."

Pitseolak looked up at Akeeagok and firmly but kindly patted his shoulder. Akeeagok gripped his hand and held it tightly, reassuringly, and gave him a warm, comforting smile. There was a bond between them, perhaps freshly kindled but solid and comforting. I watched without moving.

When Pitseolak spoke again, there was restrained excitement in his voice: "Then, the next day, I talked to Akeeagok. He said that he would teach me how to hunt and how to live in the snow. He said he would help me to learn about how to shoot seal and find caribou — all those things I cannot do."

He released his hand from Akeeagok's shoulder, cupped both hands between his knees, and gave me a fixed stare. He was now like a student who had come to the end of a complicated equation and was hesitating before telling his tutor the answer. His face was gaunt with emotional tension, and his eyelids twitched. He swallowed and then spoke.

"You see, I have decided everything now. I know what I want to do." There was pleading in his eyes. He wanted it to be right. "I want to become an Eskimo again."

I drew heavily on my cigarette and then let the smoke trickle out randomly through my fingers. For a moment, I didn't know what to say, but I knew that he wanted me to speak. It was as if I had forgotten all the words I had ever learned. Our eyes were clamped towards one another. He was waiting.

I took a quick drag and exhaled with one brief, efficient blow. "Pitseolak," I said. "If you believe that this is right, if you think that this is what you really want to do, then I also believe it is right for you."

He smiled, nodded, and said, "Thank you." Akeeagok seemed to be saying the same.

I smiled back at Pitseolak, aware that I was watching the embryo of a personal freedom. I hoped I would still be around when it matured into total confidence.

Twelve

Snowballs were hitting the bedroom window, their gentle clomp! clomp! gradually waking us out of a deep sleep.

"Snowballs," Jill casually observed.

"Yes, I can hear them."

"Who is it?"

"Haven't the slightest idea."

They persisted for a short while longer.

"Better go and see who it is," I suggested, snuggling deeper into the covers. Neither of us was eager to get up. The heating system had gone off several hours ago, and within that short period of time the temperature of the house had dropped from a comfortable 80° F to a severe -20° F.

"You'd better go and see. Might be something important," I encouraged. Blearily, Jill dressed beneath the blankets and then trotted out and across the living room. The doors were opened for the minimum amount of time, were rapidly slammed again, and I could hear her talking: "Now, if you had gone away and studied this sort of thing, you could come to fix it all for us!" She was joking with Pitseolak.

I inched deeper into the warmth, then decided I was being impolite, and sprang out of bed before I had the chance to reconsider such a brazen act. The room was absolutely freezing. I grabbed a handful of clothing and dressed hurriedly, throwing on garments at random. I promptly regretted my enthusiasm. Whereas the bedroom had been like a refrigerator, the larger open-plan dining room resembled a deep freeze. I donned a woollen hat and a pair of mittens, which someone had left on the sideboard the previous night, and then ventured forth to meet Pitseolak. Jill rapidly departed in the opposite direction, her teeth chattering.

"What's the matter?" Pitseolak asked sarcastically. "It's not cold! Look — no gloves, no parka hood!"

"Very clever! But why are you wearing four sweaters, three pairs of trousers, and those caribou kamiks?"

He glanced down at his feet, conceded the point, and offered: "There's a bit of a chilly wind outside."

"My god, Pitseolak! It's blinking cold in here when that furnace goes off in the middle of the night!"

I pranced past him and hurried down to the furnace room. Occupying as much as one-fifth of the entire house area, this vital source of heat could sometimes be reactivated by resetting a strategic jump switch which triggered itself off in response to the fluctuations of the fuel discharge system. The red button, I was delighted to note, was in the right position. I depressed the green one above it and heard that adorable droning which meant that warm air would again be rushing through the lattice of tubes which webbed the inner walls and flooring. Then I went back to the living room.

"Give me a moment to get myself back in order," I said, swinging my arms backwards and forwards, up and down, across and around my torso.

Pitseolak sauntered to the window, fingered a crack in the curtain, and with well-contemplated antagonism remarked, "Nice day. Not a cloud in the sky."

"Well, go and sit outside in it then while I get the coffee

on." He laughed, and we all went into the kitchen, knowing that the gathering heat would exit there first. I threw some chairs around the old open oven and soon the three of us were warming ourselves with mugs of last night's coffee dregs. A fresh pot was on the ring, brewing.

"Now, what brings an honest, decent citizen such as yourself pestering us respectable folk at such a ridiculous hour on a Saturday morning?"

"I'm going hunting," he declared.

"Congratulations!" I retorted, flapping a mitten. "Well, now that I'm abreast of the latest news, perhaps I can retire to my well-deserved weekend lie-in?"

I made as if to rise and added mockingly: "I hope you'll be very happy."

"I'm sure I will. Thank you."

It was the sort of repartee we often indulged in, but Jill yanked my sleeve.

"Where are you going?" I asked. "Presumably with Akeeagok?"

"Yes, he's taking me to the floe edge to hunt seal."

"Have you been out there before?"

"No. At least, not for a very long time."

"We went there some months back with Eteloo in the bombardier," said Jill. "Really beautiful."

It had indeed been beautiful: first, the craggy undulating snow-clad boulders, then the flat sea ice, and suddenly a wavy line of blue where the sea appeared. It had struck me as spectacular, and I still hold it to be among the most impressive views I have ever seen, the deep, rich blue of the Hudson Strait stretching like some carefully placed line across an artist's white canvas.

"How are you going? Skidoo?"

"Yes. Akeeagok is taking his father's skidoo and sled. We'll be gone all day. The other hunters say that there are masses of seals out there at the moment." He hesitated, then with rising excitement added: "We'll get the lot between the two of us!"

We all knew that it was ambition speaking. When Jill and I had made our trip to the floe edge, Eteloo had had to point to the bobbing seals' heads at least half a dozen times before I saw even one of them, despite their surprising closeness. Seals only need a matter of seconds to surface and take in air before sinking below again. Watching their agility, I had marvelled at the sharpness of reflex and keenness of eye required to see one, aim, and shoot it — all before it bobbed out of sight again.

"Akeeagok already has a canoe out there, and we'll paddle around in the water just off the edge and hope to get the seals at close range," said Pitseolak. There was a touch of naivety in his voice, but I knew that he was slightly nervous about this, his first trip as a hunter. He desperately needed to shoot something and confirm to himself that he was going to make it after all.

"Well, we wish you luck," I said.

"And if you don't see any today, then there's always another day," added Jill deliberately.

"Well, actually, I came to ask you if you had any bullets I can buy from you or borrow." From my detailed description of our own hunting trip, Pitseolak knew full well that I still had almost a full box of bullets somewhere in the house.

"Sure! Over there on the end of the bookcase. Middle shelf. Take the lot."

"Thanks. I'll replace them."

"Don't bother. I don't even understand those things anyway! Let us know how you make out."

Then he was gone, running through the biting cold wind.

"I hope that he gets something," remarked Jill, a trifle ominously. I grimaced agreement.

We sat quietly for a minute or so, thinking about the established route that the pair would be taking: down in front of the Hudson's Bay store; turn right over the hummocky ice along the shoreline, then on and out, past the refuse tip with its white gulls hovering like vultures over the pickings; then the more-or-less straight route, out for ten to fifteen miles to the floe edge itself.

"Do you know it's only six-fifteen?" I commented casually.

"A hard life! What do you fancy for breakfast?"

Mangitak told me that the two young men expected to be back by about five in the evening, although without watches such times were always determined by the movement and depth of shadows as the sun worked its path towards another corner of the earth. Nevertheless, that evening Jill and I sat looking at the panoramic view from about four o'clock on, and by seven decided that we had either missed them or they had indeed caught so many seals that they were forced to travel much more slowly than normal. At eight-thirty it was a typically clear crisp Arctic night, and we ambled outside for a stroll in the hope of catching a brief performance of the Northern Lights. We then met a rather agitated Oshoochiak.

"Pitseolak's not back yet," he said. He walked quickly away in the direction of Mangitak's house. We watched him go in, and then shortly afterwards they both appeared.

"What's happening?" I called.

"My brother is not back yet from his hunting trip, and we are worried," said Mangitak. "We're off to see Oshaweetok and then maybe Policee."

It was a common and sensible practice for all hunters to let Oshaweetok know of their plans before setting off on a hunting trip, for he was one of the most respected hunters in the settlement. If he was out, then the local Mountie (known by all as Policee) always knew roughly who was where so that if a party was long overdue, a search could then be organized. The non-return of the two young men was now causing some mild concern, and we too began to feel a slight anxiety.

Anything could have happened out in the tundra, miles from everywhere. Days and weeks passed sometimes without seeing another soul or moving object. It is eerie to be faced with such total isolation. Although Akeeagok was experienced, he was also relatively young to be taking along someone who might very well prove to be an inept liability, such as I might have been. At the same time, I reasoned that the way to and from the floe edge — presuming that they had taken the conventional tracks — always had a great deal of traffic each day, and no one could possibly break down or get into any form of trouble without being noticed.

Jill and I discussed it all and decided that we were over-reacting. After a couple of hours, we retired for the night, feeling that as likely as not Pitseolak would wake us up in the morning with more snowballs at the window — at a similarly unearthly hour — to report on his outing.

We gave it all only a passing thought next morning, and after tidying up around the house we both settled down to while away another peaceful Sunday. At roughly eleven o'clock, Mangitak peered through the front window, his breath freezing onto the pane in a pattern of tiny radiating crystals. His eyes shifted around the room and I lip-read: "Is Pitseolak here?"

"No!" I shouted, shaking my head.

He frowned, shrugged his shoulders and disappeared.

"Heck! He hasn't come back yet!" I said to Jill.

I threw on some clothes and ran out into the snow in pursuit of Mangitak. Some distance from the house, I noticed the local Mountie emerging from Oshaweetok's doorway, his usual calm humorous air replaced by something more businesslike and serious.

"Hey, Policee! What's all this about Pitseolak?" I yelled. But he didn't hear me.

I next saw Akeeagok's father. He was carrying a rifle and striding towards Oshoochiak's house.

"Akeeagok?" I asked.

"I don't know."

The situation was obviously getting very serious. He hurried off, and within minutes, it seemed, a search party was assembled. Soon, several skidoos were heading across the ice towards the distant floe edge. Anxiously, Jill and I watched them go. We remained tense for the rest of the day, wishing that we too owned a skidoo so that we could be doing something more positive than mooning anxiously about the house.

"We looked everywhere for them," explained Mangitak that night. "No, nothing." He spoke calmly but was clearly distraught and tired. "We went the normal way to the floe edge, some of the others keeping right along the shore so that they could look into bays and behind boulders where the two might, for some reason, have decided to rest. And then, at the edge, we went off in both directions for many miles without seeing any signs of them. Two groups then went all the way along to Catherine Bay to ask Kaka whether he had seen Akeeagok and Pitseolak. It was from him that we got the news."

I sensed the worst. "What did he say?"

"He said that yesterday, in the late afternoon, Inookee was looking out from his house at camp when he saw a canoe drifting by, some miles out to sea. When he saw that nobody was in it, he hooked up his dog team and komatik, and then he and Kaka went to catch it. No one was in the canoe when they got to it, just two rifles resting across the seat in the middle."

135

When Mangitak spoke again, it was with the fatalism I had so often noticed in the Inuit, an almost casual acceptance of disaster. "I think maybe Pitseolak is dead. Maybe drowned."

The discovery of the empty canoe was certainly ominous. Possibly a walrus had surfaced and toppled them overboard — although, in this case, one would hardly have expected the rifles to have remained so carefully balanced in the middle of the boat. There seemed very little point in speculating what might have occurred. In the stillness of those Arctic waters anything could happen; once immersed in the water, the two young men would freeze to death within minutes. I remembered being told of a local hunter who, after hopelessly flapping in the sea for a brief spell, had deliberately drowned himself because he knew that this was preferable to freezing. Fatalistic, but also harshly realistic.

Nevertheless, I was not as pessimistic as Mangitak. After all, I told myself, Akeeagok's own father had only recently fallen through some weak ice at the floe edge, and with the clear determination to survive, he had clambered out and galloped back into the settlement — always managing to keep his body temperature just above that fatal line. But all these reflective asides still left Pitseolak without a rifle, transport, or food, out in the tundra now for two days. And he didn't have the experience and knowledge of Akeeagok's father.

Special prayers were said at church that night; and Tukpungi, whose house they would have to pass first should they return, undertook to keep a vigil. Mangitak sat quietly in a chair, apparently resigned to having lost a brother.

As dawn broke on Monday morning, the entire community was curiously alert, eager for something new, something, anything, which might cast an explanation on the whereabouts of the two missing men. But there was still no news; nothing further to add to what had been gleaned yesterday. Although the hunters once more set off for the floe edge, this time they were merely keeping their eyes trimmed for anything unusual, rather than specifically going out to search. They had families to feed, and no more time could be spent unproductively. They had to eat.

The mood around the school was also different, and the children were pensively calm and quiet. Martha wasn't there. Respectfully, the topic was barely broached. It must have been almost noon when the mood was suddenly shattered. From somewhere outside, we heard rifles being shot — a burst of gunfire like that of a brief volley. Simultaneously, the school bell rang, and everyone leapt into the cold flurries and charged towards the coastline.

We stood there not knowing what it might mean. The last time such blasting had been heard was before Christmas, when it had heralded the arrival of a group of Eskimos who had journeyed by open boat for a week or so all the way from Arctic Quebec, on the other side of the straits. The present volley could therefore mean anything, although all of us assumed that it had some connection with the missing men — either good or bad. We waited expectantly for half an hour, but there were no further developments. Gradually, it dawned on me that the shots could have come from miles away, for sound travels endlessly in this tranquil land. The party might be at least another hour or two before coming into view.

Back at work that afternoon, time passed laboriously. The echoing rat-a-tat-tat had occurred an eternity ago, and, in the absence of further explanation, the atmosphere was fretfully anxious. Martha was still absent, though that could mean she merely had a cold. In any case, the whole noisy mystery might prove to have no connection with her brother.

At four o'clock I went to the store for some cigarettes. "They're back," nonchalantly remarked the manager, almost as an aside. He was a longtime resident of the North who had seen so many disasters and dramas that he had become almost immune to worry.

"What happened?" I asked, relief speaking on my behalf.

"Silly little devils lost their canoe and had to walk back!" He shook his head in disbelief. He served the next customer.

I hurried home, thinking that Jill might still be in ignorance of the outcome, and as I slipped and slithered along the track that led to the top of the hill I suddenly saw Pitseolak charging down the adjacent slope. He was bounding across the snow like a child rushing into the breakers of the sea.

"Hi!" he said as he slid to a halt, bumping into my shoulder. The jolt, if nothing else, served to confirm that he was not a figment of my imagination.

"Where the hell have you been?" I said. I had never before met someone whom I believed to be returned from the dead, and I had thus not rehearsed any monumental words for the occasion.

He laughed the same old laugh. I playfully punched his arm and said, "Don't play games like that again! Okay?" Then we jogged up to tell Jill.

Comfortably settled in his favourite armchair, Pitseolak told us what had happened. Although his tale was simple, I realized that the details were of great significance, especially to him.

"We shot a great many seal," he began, "and paddled to the ice so that we could rest them down before going back for more. While we were dragging them to a safe place some distance inland, the canoe broke away and started to drift. We tried everything to get it back, but the rope was very short and we couldn't grip it. It went farther and farther away. So we decided to follow it, hoping that somewhere farther along the floe edge it would change direction and come back so that we could grab it. But it didn't.

"We followed it for many miles, and when it was night, we went over to Alareak Island and hoped that it might beach itself nearby in the morning. The tides were heading that way. That night we didn't eat anything. We had no matches and only one penknife between us. Our rifles we had left on the seat of the canoe. So we buried ourselves in the snow and waited for light again.

"If you bury yourself in the loose snow, you know, it's quite warm." He spoke now as an expert. "Anyhow, when we got up the next morning — really only a couple of hours later — we realized that the current had taken the canoe somewhere else and that we had lost it. We were left without anything. Akeeagok then said that we were many miles from Cape Dorset and that we would have to get back as soon as possible. To keep warm, we ran a little and walked a little, jumping whenever we felt too cold. By walking, running, then jumping, we didn't get too tired and we could go for many miles without having to stop.

"Once or twice, we stopped for a mouthful of snow, but it is very cold for the stomach and can make you ill. It doesn't really help to quench the thirst either — in fact, too much will make you even thirstier."

Pitseolak was talking with confidence, like some venerable raconteur who has told stories for years to the gathered young. We listened to the saga, completely mesmerized.

"Then we started to get hungry. On the sea ice we knew that we could find walrus and seal — but you can't get them with just a pocketknife. So we cut back towards the land to look for some hare or lemming. Akeeagok caught a small white hare; he trapped it by a hole and stabbed it. Then we skinned it and ate the meat. It tasted very good. And then we walked again, ran, and jumped. And when we got cold, we went into the snow for a while and got warm again."

"But how come you didn't meet any of the people who were out looking for you?" I couldn't help asking. "They seemed to have searched everywhere, as far as I can make out."

"Well, yes, we did once see their skidoos moving in the distance, but they were too far away to see us. You see, we started to walk along the sea ice but this was a very long way back; it would have taken us many miles more and there would be no food along the way. So we went up into the mountains. We knew that nobody would see us, but it was much quicker to come back that way. We then came back down onto the sea ice once more somewhere near Peter Pitseolak's old camp — and soon afterwards we met the men coming back into Cape Dorset."

"When did you get back?" Jill asked.

"The middle of this afternoon."

I took a long look at him. It was the legendary tale of man alone against nature. Almost incredibly, Pitseolak had won.

"Amazing!" I exhaled, somewhat dumbstruck. Then, shaking his hand, I added, "You're bloody amazing!"

He grinned. "I know," he replied with that familiar blend of conceit and pride. "But I am an Eskimo, you know." He paused, before adding, "And I'll make a good hunter, too!"

I now didn't doubt him.

Thirteen

Pitseolak had never had the passion for card-playing that obsessed many of the hunters, and I think he had only come to watch the game in Jaw's house because he lacked anything better to do. My own reasons for being there were much the same. Making my way slowly up the hill the following week, after a bit of shopping at the Bay, I had run into Mr. Munarmeekudluk who had redirected my course. "Come on!" he had said. "Let's watch them playing cards." I was more than willing. Although I didn't understand the intricacies of the game, I was always fascinated by the self-willed intensity that seemed to be an essential ingredient. Cards would be snatched rapidly from a diminishing pile in the centre, then carefully placed at the bottom of the stacks that the players treasured in their hands. Cautiously, they would be unfurled, but only so that the tiniest edge became visible, scarcely revealing the symbol of the suit. There was a deliberately connived mystery about the whole thing.

Mr. Munarmeekudluk barged in on the intense scene with a total lack of reverence. Like some comic character in a Victorian music hall, he danced around the ring of players, rustling hair, jerking parka hoods, and ending his act with a quick two-step into the heap of money and cards. Then he hopped away, laughing uproariously. I was so preoccupied with trying to disassociate myself from his antics that I didn't notice Pitseolak at first. But I did realize that several glances registered my presence.

I stationed myself behind Tytoosie, keeping what I thought was an unobtrusive distance away for fear of putting him off his stride. He grabbed his own top card and with a vicious thrust smacked it into the deck. Then he fingered his way towards the pack, flicked one off the top, and cradled it in his palm. Again, I watched the cautious and ceremonial unfurling of the bent cards curved between his fingers. A club surfaced — the jack.

"Tornwa!" shouted Tytoosie, turning round and snarling at me. "Tornwa! Tornwa!" Then he and everyone laughed. Against the wall, Munarmeekudluk slapped his hands — the cymbals — and let out a hearty guffaw.

"What's he saying?" I pleaded. "What's the word mean?"

"Tornwa!" I heard another player saying derisively towards Tytoosie.

Mr. Munarmeekudluk was short of breath from his chortling and could only bleat, "Tornwa — that's you, lad! You're Tytoosie's tornwa!" With another guffaw, he wobbled backwards out of control, his mouth wide open and his head high into the air.

I urgently looked around the room, wondering if I had committed some sort of cardinal sin by peering over Tytoosie's shoulder. Perhaps he thought I was relaying the contents of his hand to someone on the other side of the ring. The last thing I wanted was to become involved in some form of cheating scandal. It was then that I noticed Pitseolak standing by the rear door. He was leaning against the woodwork, biting his nails in a bored manner.

"What's it all mean?" I shouted to him, making my way around the scattering of bodies as I spoke.

"Don't worry about it," he said, sweeping back the sides of his hair with his hands. "Tytoosie says that you're a ghost, a ghost that is bringing him bad luck." His head swivelled towards the card player as he spoke, and their grins met. "But now you've gone, he says that Munar-meekudluk is a tornwa."

I glanced back at my satanical counterpart. He was flopping on the floor, oblivious to the charges, reading a comic book that he had snatched from his young daughter.

"Come! Let's go and have a cup of coffee in my house," Pitseolak suggested, already leading the way to the door. "I don't really like this card-playing business anyway. Seems wrong to me," he added moralistically.

As we crunched along between the houses, I asked, "Why are they so serious about these games? I mean, I know that the particular game has quite a lot of money going on it, but why this half-hearted superstitious reference to tornwas?"

"Oh, I don't know. Sometimes I don't understand them myself!" I was surprised to hear Pitseolak saying "them" again. Temporarily, he seemed to have alienated himself from the world he had deliberately joined.

In his house, we sat drinking instant coffee from chipped enamel mugs, lounging on the floor, idly listening to some scratchy sounds that emanated from his portable record player. Unprotected records lay here and there around the house. An early Gordon Lightfoot 45 had been burnt with a cigarette, others were chipped, and most were characterized by innumerable scratches.

"See!" Pitseolak said in controlled disgust, "I just can't keep any of my things to myself around here!" He span a record across the room as if it was a discus. "Another one useless!"

"I still can't get over Tytoosie calling me an evil ghost," I commented, "even if he didn't really mean it as anything other than an excuse."

"Well, it was partly an excuse. But, you see, deep down

he probably also saw you as a possible cause of the bad card."

"That's ridiculous!"

"Maybe," Pitseolak said, shaking his head. "But just remember that we live in a part of the world where many things happen that we cannot explain — the weather, luck in hunting, sometimes death. And so there always has to be some sort of explanation for these happenings, and many people simply explain them away as being the work of a tornwa. Shifting blame, if you like. Trying to make someone or something responsible."

"Do you actually believe in all of this tornwa business yourself?" I asked.

"Ha! Not really, but then strange things do happen, you know, which none of us seem to be able to explain."

He hesitated, partly as if he didn't want to continue and also as if weighing up whether it was worth the time in bothering to talk about it.

"Go on!" I urged. "Tell me some of the strange things you have seen or heard of happening to people around here." I was intrigued that Pitseolak the cynic, who had been so sceptical when I had first told him about Keelut, had obviously been taking an interest in such matters — though he hastened to assure me that he was only repeating what others had told him.

I accepted the terms and qualification. He looked at me doubtfully for a moment and then said, "Well, for example, there was this young boy living out at a camp one summer in the area of Andrew Gordon Bay, as you call it. He says that he caught a long, black thing like a worm with legs. He says that it was about ten inches long. It had a big mouth, and when it opened its mouth it had two big black tusks coming down. He says that they caught it but didn't know what it was." Pitseolak looked up to test my reaction. Seeing my interest, he continued, "Later that week, so he tells us, they saw a very long fish, longer than they had ever seen before, and it swam faster than anything they'd ever seen before. But they didn't catch it because it swam through the net." Pitseolak looked at me once more. "You see, these are two things which they say they saw — and no one knows who or what they were. Could be tornwas," he added with a smile, cocking his head.

"Could be," I supported. "What else?"

"Well, there are lots of stories. Some of the people have said that Echalook was out in his boat one day when he saw a big monster that looked something like an oil drum with eyes!"

"Did he shoot it?"

"No. I think he was probably very scared and came back to shore again. He left his boat just down by the house near the Brownie's hut and came straight back home." Pitseolak paused and then added, "All of this sounds ridiculous in a way, but who knows what it was? It might have been a floating oil drum. On the other hand, it might have been something like a monster — we don't know all of the animals that live in the sea, do we?"

"No. The oceanographers are always finding something new. Who knows?"

Reassured, he moved on to another story. "One family told me that they were out at camp near Chorkbak Inlet. They were by the water, looking along the beach. Then, out of the sea came a very large seal which had the face of an Eskimo. The father of the family got his gun, but the thing shouted, 'Don't shoot me.' They said it was very big, but was like a seal. So they didn't shoot, and the thing went away and they never saw it again."

Pitseolak was now enjoying relating these oddities of the tundra, and I remember thinking that one day he would recount strange personal experiences of his own with equal relish.

"You know," he continued, "just the other night, I heard two boys talking about something they had seen up on top of the hill by the Community Hall. I heard young Simionik say that he'd seen a ghost that looked like his mother drifting above him in a cloud. But his mother wasn't dead. He called out to see if it was his mother, but it just slowly faded away and they didn't see it again. Then I also heard Adamie saying that when he was out at camp near Catherine Bay, he suddenly saw a rifle floating in the air in front of him. Then it started to shoot at him, so he ran away. When he turned around again, it wasn't there — only something that looked a bit like a brown owl in its place!" Pitseolak curled his lips downwards and raised his eyebrows.

"How true do you think these are?" I asked. I was genuinely curious.

"Who knows! All I know is that this is what some people say they have seen."

He couldn't stop recalling these tales and descriptions, and I didn't try to stop him because they were coming at such a pace that he couldn't possibly have been making them up.

"Some people say that an uncle of mine had a fight with a big monster which had a pouch on its back. I've never asked him about that. I wasn't here at the time, so I don't know about it other than they say the pouch was for carrying people away. It climbed on his back and he threw it off. Then he tried to shoot it, but it suddenly disappeared. Then there has sometimes been seen an enormous bird flying on the slopes of Kingnait. They say that it looks like an eagle and has a seven-foot wing span. Someone once told me a story about it landing many years ago and taking a small boy away with it."

He rose and gestured me to the window. "They say that it comes down right over there, but I've never seen it myself." He pointed beyond the hills. Then he shrugged his shoulders and stretched out once more on the floor. "Of course, these things don't just happen here, you know. When I was in Frobisher on that course for engineering, I met a man from Clyde River who said that a man there had seen a long creature that was like a snake. He saw it when he was hunting seal. He was also a carver, so when he got back home he made a carving of the thing he had seen, but no one had any idea what it was. I don't know what happened to the carving — maybe he still has it."

I lit a cigarette, he didn't want one, and as I blew smoke into the air, he asked, "What do you think about these stories? I mean, do you think that they are all made up by everyone? Do they all sound silly to you?"

"Quite frankly, Pitseolak, I have never heard anything like these before, although perhaps you are close to the truth when you say that man might never know of the things in the sea. I do know that microscopic organisms are frequently dredged from the depths which are not classified, or even classifiable. So maybe there are some odd things swimming around up here which no one knows about."

Pitseolak looked relieved that I wasn't dismissing the tales as rubbish. "We were talking about tornwas, at first," he said. "Well, let me tell you something strange that happened when my mother Kanikpellik died. One old man had a dream in Cape Dorset that week in which he was told that two people would die in this place that same week. The man did not know from his dream who these two people would be, but he did say that one of them would be a woman and the other would be a young boy. As you know, his dream came true, although we did not think it would." I shrugged. Maybe coincidence. Maybe not.

"Another thing that happened to my mother is also odd," said Pitseolak. "This was when she was in hospital before she died. She told me that she was in bed one night when she felt somebody's hands pushing down on her stomach. She thought it was the nurse, but when she woke up and saw nobody there, she screamed. That very next morning, she released herself from the nursing station and came home. There are many people who say that nursing station is haunted by ghosts, because it was built on the site of an old graveyard which was used by people who lived here many years ago, before there was a big settlement here like there is now. I do know that my mother told me all these things herself and that she believed that it did happen to her. This story I really do believe because it was my own mother who told me about it."

I didn't speak; and Pitseolak, too, became silent. I had heard a corroborating story of these mysterious pressing hands. The nursing staff were good friends of ours, and we often entertained one another either in our house or in their nursing station quarters. At dinner one night, we had been discussing the old graveyard which lay about five feet beneath the plateful of roast beef I was at that moment eating. The male nurse commented that it had been a source of difficulty at first, because many people were reluctant to attend a clinic that desecrated the burial ground. One could not help but wonder if some other site could have been found without having to disturb an area sacred to the local people.

"They say it's haunted," said the male nurse, with a nervous chuckle. "Actually, so do I!" He looked over to his wife. She poured gravy over the Yorkshire pudding, smiled, and said to him, "Go on! Tell them!"

He laughed again before saying, "Well, I feel daft really, but you can believe this, or believe it not. One night, I just couldn't sleep, so rather than disturb this good lady who is my wife, I went into one of the wards and clambered into one of the beds down there. Well, I had been lying on my stomach for perhaps half an hour when I felt these hands pushing down on my back. I thought it was Audrey, so I made the appropriate moans of pleasure and waited for her to make the next move. But when I turned over, she wasn't there, so I called out. She didn't answer me and when I went to the bedroom I found that she was fast asleep. I quickly ran back and checked all the doors, thinking someone was having a game with me, but they were all closed and the cupboards too. I even looked under the beds and inside the medicine cabinets. There was no one there. And this one was still snoring through it all!" His thumb curled towards his wife.

It was certainly very similar to the experience of Pitseolak's mother.

"Were you in Frobisher when they were seeing flying saucers?" I asked him.

"No, I was here for Christmas and missed it all. Heard about it, though."

That, too, was a curious story, and I still wasn't sure what to make of it. A group of young school children at Apex, over the hill from Frobisher proper, had seen a strange object out on the ice and had told their teachers about it. The teachers were interested and asked the children to draw what they had seen. In the meantime, a teacher at the main Frobisher school, several miles away, telephoned the school to say that his students had also seen something hovering far out on the ice up Cumberland Sound, and he too asked the children to draw the object.

That evening, the teachers got together and compared the drawings. All pictures clearly indicated an elongated object with some sort of sparky emissions bursting from the bottom. All the children agreed that the object had something glowing on top — some had drawn a cross, others a golden ball. But the significant thing about the drawings was that the Apex children had drawn the object so that it was fully visible from side to side, while the Frobisher students had shown it as being only partially visible, saying that it was partly obscured by a rocky promontory that was jutting out into the Sound from where they had been standing. Such a subtlety made it unlikely that there had been collusion between the two groups of students; they weren't conniving at an elaborate hoax; they had simply drawn what they had apparently seen.

In any case, several adults had had unusual experiences that night. One of the teachers at Apex told me she had been woken at about three in the morning by the hum of what she thought was a snowplough. She had assumed it was clearing the street around her house. But, next morning, she found that no snow-clearing equipment had been used. Then there was the electrical engineer at one of the main transmission centres on the hillside. He reported in his log that at about three that morning all the dials and indicators started to behave irregularly. He went outside, thinking that a cable had broken, and saw a bright glow hovering virtually overhead. After a few minutes, the glow and lights faded, and his equipment returned to normal. It was also on that same night that an airline pilot spotted a fast-flying object on his radar. Since he was near the DEW line sites, he radioed the information to the Frobisher control tower, but scarcely had he done so than the object shot off his screen. All of this was duly reported and recorded.

Pitseolak found the whole thing as odd as I did, and he told me of a similar phenomenon that had happened many years ago. An elderly man and his son, he said, had been out hunting on the ice when a bright light came to rest nearby. As they watched, they saw some little things moving around the bottom of the light; and then, after about five minutes, the light suddenly rose into the clouds and was never seen again.

"Were they terrified?" I asked. "What did they do?"

Pitseolak laughed. "I don't think they were even surprised. You must realize that around that time there were many other strange things happening to the Inuit. Planes and helicopters began appearing out of the sky when hunters didn't expect them. And they would find supply dumps in the middle of their traplines, without knowing who had put them there or when. This man and his son just dismissed the bright light as another of the oddities the kadloonas were bringing with them. Actually, I know the son. He's now a prominent member of the Frobisher Bay community, and he swears he really did see that strange light."

I wondered if he also swore to seeing the little green men — or whatever the things were moving around the base of the light. It all seemed rather far fetched, though no more inexplicable — when I thought about it — than what the school children had apparently seen. As for Tytoosie's tornwa and the business about ghosts and giant sea-worms, was it all a big joke, an elaborately embroidered pattern of light relief? Possibly, but not probably, I decided.

The isolation of the tundra is a very fertile environment for superstitions to breed; and there is something about the very nature of the Inuit culture, with its unpredictability, that makes the emergence of a fantasy world inevitable, almost a conscious escape from reality. I didn't find it odd that Pitseolak had never asked his uncle about the pouched creature with whom he was said to have struggled. Obviously, Pitseolak didn't want to break the spèll, to shatter the illusion. It was the same reaction as my own unwillingness to admit that there might be no Loch Ness monster; Nessie was part of my fantasy world (I have always wanted the creature to be proved a reality). As for the tornwa, it was a perfectly valid way of explaining the inexplicable. I have always felt that scientists will one day resolve all the unknowns, including ghost stories — which are by no means confined to the Arctic — and ghostly hands in old cemeteries. I reckoned that, for the Eskimos, the tornwa occupied much the same position as my scientists.

As Pitseolak and I sat companionably together, exploring age-old mysteries from his culture as we played modern records from mine, I lost all sense of time. But suddenly I realized that at least four hours must have passed since I had left my house to do a quick bit of shopping.

"Heavens! I've got to rush!" I said.

"Why?"

"It must be long past supper time. Jill is probably going out of her mind trying to keep my meal warm. And she's got her Brownie pack this evening. She won't be too pleased if she has to wait supper for me."

"Strange ways you have," said Pitseolak. His voice was mocking. Although he knew I had to leave, he couldn't see that it mattered if I ate a hot or cold meal, and whether I ate it now or later. Since abandoning his mechanic's training, fixed times, schedules, and routines had become a thing of the past. He no longer wore his watch. It had been discarded along with the shaving lotion.

"See you," I said, giving his boot a retaliatory poke.

He laughed, flapping his arms teasingly in hurry-hurry gestures as I threw on my parka. In spite of the growing identification with his own people, he was basically the same old Pitseolak.

Fourteen

Over the weeks, he changed — not gently and slowly, but radically, abruptly. He had chosen his path and now pursued it with vigour, confidently stepping through its maze of hardships, casually shrugging aside its testing demands.

His appearance, too, was different, unrestricted by rigid conventions and utterly free to the whims of comfort and convenience. His hair was longer, shaggy, and unkempt; there was still a sheen to its colouring, but this was the result of constant sweat, exposure, and greasy hands. The carefully groomed complexion was now darker, battered into a deeper shade by the wind, cold, and snow — much more rugged, less delicate. His skin was dry, chafed, and hardened, with deep creases radiating from the corners of his eyes and mouth, etched there by the continual straining and wincing demanded of thoughtless elements.

"Here, have this!" he said one evening, waving a chunk of frozen caribou at me. He then looked back over his shoulder and spoke at length to Akeeagok in Eskimo — in a way, as if I wasn't even there.

"We've plenty. Had a good hunt," he added, having turned briefly and found me still standing there clutching the meat. The words were in accurate anticipation of my intended protests that their own families might need it more than I.

"Thanks!" I remarked, squeezing past them to get to the large deep freeze which we kept in the storeroom between the outer and inner doors. As I returned, they side-stepped slightly to let me pass, but their conversation went on without interruption, and neither bothered to break off and look at me.

I stood back a little watching, waiting to be invited to join. They seemed to have forgotten that I was there. It was rather strange and unfamiliar, and I didn't know how to react, so I simply lingered awkwardly and patiently, trying to catch the odd word here and there. And as I hovered, I gradually realized that I was in the presence of two hunters who had merely thought to share their catch with me; this was no longer Pitseolak popping in for a chat over the usual cup of coffee, but a young Eskimo proud of his success and eager to give some of it away to a friend who couldn't hunt.

I glanced at his clothing and found it difficult to equate the well-worn parka as being the same one which he had proudly brought back from Frobisher Bay barely a month earlier. It was dirty and stained, and the flamboyant, bright red-and-yellow trimming had now become a blurred pattern of maroon and dull murky orange. His wildly gesticulating hands were cracked and unwashed from the past week's hunting, the nails black and broken.

"We went all the way to the southern edge of Amadjuak," he said, catching me by complete surprise. But in that single sentence I saw once again the same genuine smile and the enthusiasm that he would never again lose.

"Well, sit down and tell me all about it!" I motioned to the chairs. "No point in the pair of you huddling into the corner and blabbering in Eskimo when you know that I haven't the slightest idea of what you are on about!"

They both laughed and nestled into the offered comfort.

"Sorry," apologized Pitseolak, "but we were just talking

about the lead stag which I should have got with one shot. Instead, I missed it altogether and we then spent the best part of the afternoon trying to chase the entire herd while it regrouped."

He shrugged his shoulders and winked at Akeeagok. "But we got them in the end!"

"Okay, then let's hear about it! When did you arrive back?"

"About an hour ago." Instinctively he fondled his wrist for the watch that was no longer there. "Yes, about an hour ago I guess."

Ever since that first chilly morning when he had come to borrow bullets, he had made it a practice to come over as soon as he returned from a trip. It was perhaps his way of sharing something of himself, or maybe a subconscious desire to report on his progress. He enjoyed talking about his new life, knowing that I wouldn't become bored or disinterested. It enabled our friendship to endure this strange transitional period through which his life was passing; we could continue to sit and chat — though on his terms and within the confines of the subjects which he alone was experiencing. I often thought, with unabashed amusement, that there had occurred a peculiar reversal of roles which could scarcely have been foreseen a short while ago. It was difficult to imagine that it was he who had once eagerly prodded me to tell him of the night when Mangitak and I had gone around the houses looking for two wolves.

"After talking with Kaka and Inookee at Catherine Bay," he was saying, "we decided on the usual route up Chorkbak and on to Tessik Lake. We already knew that the caribou had long since moved eastwards, but we pursued some of the stragglers we had heard about from other hunters."

As usual, Akeeagok sat contentedly listening to this strange tongue which he had never understood or learned.

"We got several that day, skinned them, cut the carcasses,

and then buried them in one of our usual caches. You know for yourself how cold it gets up there in the middle of the lake, but we decided not to camp but head back a bit and then aim for Amadjuak."

The Plain of Amadjuak is the great breeding ground for thousands of flocks of Canada geese, and Pitseolak knew that I had long harboured a desire to go there and see it for myself, that I was forever fascinated by any stories which told of that natural reserve. It was a long journey, but he had already skirted the southern edge of this wilderness on several occasions. My eyes betrayed envy any time he mentioned the place.

"The birds are really coming in now." He tossed his head teasingly. "More and more, all the time!"

"Yes, I'm sure. I know it! I know it! Don't keep rubbing it in!"

He muttered an aside to Akeeagok, who seemed amused by the taunting. But then he became serious — and unusually eloquent.

"You know, it's really beautiful up there. I'd like to take you some day. The land is flatter and more gentle than it is along the coastal areas, and at this time of the year, when the snows are melting, you can see patches of green and mauve lichens. Around the pockets of meltwater, where it's often muddy and swampy, the tall white heads of cotton-grass are beginning to appear. And it's so quiet and peaceful, no noisy breaking of ice or the creaking of the seas which we get around here at Cape Dorset. Just the whistling of the wind, the flapping of wings overhead, and the distant sounds of nesting birds."

I felt inclined to encourage him to become a naturalist, or a wildlife writer — but hastily veered from the thought.

"We stayed there for some time," he continued, "until we had enough birds without overloading the komatik — remember that we still had to collect the meat we had left back at Tessik. Then we started to come back." He squirmed slightly in the chair. "And guess what we came across," he said. "Somewhere at the mouth of Chorkbak, but on the land side and not on the sea ice, we found an old campsite. It looked as if it might have been a Hudson's Bay trading post. There were lots of rusty tins, the large sort that army ration biscuits might come in. There were other things too, like bits of wood and circles of stone — just as if someone had been living there a long time ago."

I remembered hearing that the Hudson's Bay Company had once had a sort of informal outpost up that way. In the early years of this century, there had been several collecting stations scattered across this part of Baffin Island so that roaming bands of Eskimo could bring in the pelts they collected. The pelts were then taken to the main depots at Frobisher Bay or Cape Dorset. I suggested that Pitseolak ask his father about the campsite, for Oshoochiak had probably called there in the old days. But Pitseolak seemed not to be listening. He was delving into his pocket, trying to locate something. Then, out came his clenched fist.

"We found this there too," he said, carefully unwrapping an unseen object from a piece of rag. It was an ivory harpoon head roughly five inches long, broken at the base end but perfectly shaped into a curved point at the top. The tip had been reinforced by a piece of metal from a tin, carefully recessed into the ivory so that it became a sharp cutting edge and point. I fondled it in my hand, letting a finger probe the inside of the holes through which a string, probably a strip of seal skin, had been passed in order to fasten it to the shaft. The older hunters had used this method to spear fish and to harpoon seal. Upon impact, the head detached itself, embedded in the flesh; then, like an angler giving temporary respite to a game fish, the target was allowed to take off at the end of the trailing string until it had played itself out, at which moment the hunter would haul it back in, exhausted. The technique was still basic to many whalers.

"You really have found something of worth there, Pitseolak!" I marvelled, turning it over and over, feeling the smoothness of its surfaces, contemplating the skill of the man who had fashioned it so perfectly. I passed it across to Akeeagok. He gave it a close look and then passed it back to Pitseolak.

"Yes," said Pitseolak, "I'm quite pleased that I found this because it is a genuine bit of our past. It's history. As real as the story-myths you once told me about. You know, the man who made this must have been a very skilled hunter."

He handed it back to me and, having studied it once more, I gave it back. But he withdrew.

"No! I don't want it. You can have it."

"My god, Pitseolak! I can't take this!" I spoke loudly, with indignation and surprise. "This is yours. It's an artifact! It's valuable to you, to everyone. It is your own history — you just said that yourself!"

But he waved me away. "I don't want it. It's a present."

I thrust it back towards him again. "I just can't take it, Pitseolak. It's too important to you — you know that. It's yours!"

Finally, he looked at me firmly, seriously, his eyes locked hypnotically to mine. He spoke slowly, as one exasperated by my stupidity in not understanding what it was he was trying to convey. "I want you to have it — don't you see? I give it to you." Then calmly, yet emotionally, he said, "I want to give you a part of my culture."

I held his gift and fell silent. He turned away and faced the window and the snows outside. I didn't look back as he left, and there had been no need to speak.

I watched him trample away, realizing that he had just told me that he had become a true Eskimo again.

Fifteen

Pitseolak's new-found sense of identity gave him more than confidence, more than fulfilment. As the days passed, I realized that it was not enough for him to become a seasoned hunter knowing the ways of the Inuit today. He wanted to learn everything — about the past as well as the present.

It had been a gradual development, starting perhaps with our conversation in January, when he had shown the first glimmerings of interest in the mythical dog Keelut, and receiving a strong impetus when he had seen Peter Pitseolak's collection of memorabilia. Initially, I had consciously been feeding his interest, but now he needed no encouragement. He seemed to be gripped by a passion, reading everything he could lay his hands on and eagerly . questioning anyone who could add to his knowledge.

One night in mid-spring, when we were walking together along the sea ice, I discovered that he had been spending a great deal of time with Parr, reputedly the oldest man in the community. A relative of Pitseolak's, Parr was probably in his upper eighties, although his true age was a mystery as he had been born long before records were kept locally. In a way, he was a living legend, largely because of his artistic talents. I found it ironical that this man, who had fought the fight for the best part of his life in the snowfields and ice packs of the tundra, should now, in his twilight years, be immortalized because of the way he sat at a table and drew with felt-tipped pens.

"Parr says that our names have meanings," Pitseolak announced as we crunched our way along the shoreline. "Take Eejeevudluk, for example. You know Eejeevudluk who lives here in Cape Dorset?" I nodded. "Well, that was the name of a benevolent spirit who lived in a rock long ago, according to the myths. He looked like a little man with a black face, and it is said that when he stared, his eyes cast a strange fearful glance....Then there's the name Audlaloo, which probably comes from Aulanerk — a spirit who lived by the edge of the water. According to the story, he was always naked and cold so that when he shook to keep warm, his movements caused the waves to ripple across the seas." Pitseolak turned to me, crooking his neck slightly so as to be able to look me full in the face as we walked along. "What do you think?"

"Interesting. Any more?"

"Yes. Koodjanuk, which might also be Koolooajuk. This was the name of the spirit who was present at the creation of the world. He appeared in the form of a great black bird. Do you remember me telling you that someone here had seen a great black bird on Kingnait? Yes, well you didn't know what it meant, and neither did I at the time. Anyway, Koolooajuk was a black bird with a hooked beak and a white underbelly. And it had the power to heal the sick."

"And Parr told you this?"

"Yup."

I was excited. I had only ever spoken briefly to Parr, for he was in failing health, staying in his home most of the time, and I had never wanted to invade his privacy. "Keep talking to him, Pitseolak," I urged. "He's a man from a fading era. He knows things that others would be eager to learn about. Not just Eskimos, but people all over the world."

"I am talking to him," replied Pitseolak.

The ice was shiny, as if someone had laboriously gone over it with a high wax polish. On we walked, talking companionably, both of us realizing how much there was to be learned about the old Eskimo culture. After about an hour, we came upon a team of dogs, attached to stakes which had been driven individually into the ice, the metal spikes hammered deep beneath the surface so that even the strongest of the animals would not be able to break free. The huskies were all asleep, but as we approached they were suddenly up, pulling, straining, growling, and barking in our direction. Instinctively, I held back, but after a while they grew accustomed to our presence and gradually became silent.

The night was calm, quiet, as only a night in the Arctic can be.

"You know, I'm going to miss all this," I said.

"Yes. I'm sure you will."

I had decided to leave the Arctic for a while. During the past months, as Pitseolak had been redirecting his life, I had been doing much the same with mine. I had reached one of those critical stages when I needed to sit back and take stock of where I was going, and I knew that I could do this best somewhere else, away from here, where I would be able to take an objective view.

My association with Pitseolak had played a role in this decision. Through him, I had realized that I was becoming deeply involved with a group of people whose traditions and culture I was helping to change and perhaps destroy. The traditional Eskimo way of life was falling apart. Their happy-go-lucky philosophy had turned around like some vicious serpent and was consuming their time-honoured ways while they sat by, apparently unconcerned. It was easy to rationalize that this was inevitable and that it had been inevitable ever since Martin Frobisher had first drifted over the horizon with guns and accordions. But that didn't make it any more acceptable.

My feelings were confused, jumbled. I wanted to stay and live in the Arctic; I didn't want to leave these people who had become such close friends. But I was uncertain about the role I should be playing, and sometimes I even felt that I was an intruder; I didn't want to be there to watch the inescapable period of transition with all of its traumas and problems. And so I had decided to leave.

Over the next weeks I packed on a piecemeal basis, bit by bit, day by day, doing it carefully and meticulously but without enthusiasm. Sometimes Pitseolak joined me. He never stayed long, always a fleeting visit between hunts, for he was forever off, rifle in hand, trying to find something or merely going out back to shoot at tin cans, stones, or at the large black crows that hovered over one of the tips just below my house.

His entire being, manner, betrayed an urgency, an all but uncontrollable impulse that magnetically drew him back into the barrenness of the tundra. He was always out there trying to learn something new, to understand something else; he had a persistence that reminded me of those early boxers who fought a hundred rounds until one or the other collapsed from exhaustion. I felt that he could take on anything that might be blasted at him, that, if necessary, he would feed the entire community on his own. He was not content to be just another hunter. Sometimes he showed a frightening lust to shoot and kill anything that could be eaten. After a hard day with few rewards, his eyes appeared wild and angry; they always looked red, tired, and strained from the glaring snow.

He spoke more and more of wanting to live out in the

tundra, of getting away from the distractions of settlement life. But I knew that he was happy, at one with himself. And, of course, neither of us knew that his future would be so brief, that he had found his life only to lose it.

"He looks like a pansy!" Pitseolak chuckled one day as he sat looking through a photograph album which I was about to pack. I glanced over his shoulder and saw that he was looking at a picture of himself taken several months before.

"Perhaps a playboy?" I suggested more accurately.

He cocked his head to one side, peered again at the colour print. "Perhaps. Yes. Could I ever have looked like that? Christ!"

"In different times, my friend, in different times." He gave me a grin — the passing glimmer of his predecessor — then picked his nose.

"At least this other guy washed," I chided gently. "Get yourself up, little brother, and nip into the other room and have a bath on us." I could talk to him like this without causing offence, but he didn't take the hint.

"Another time," he replied. Other hunters had always said the same.

The packing of our accumulated possessions became an endless chore, interrupted only by the welcome appearance of visitors at the door. This was also a hectic period throughout the entire settlement, with the election of various officers to serve on several local committees. Pitseolak's father, Oshoochiak, was elected onto both the Community Hall Council and the Community Council, the latter body operating under the auspices of the Mission House.

Pitseolak hadn't bothered to vote in either election. "Load of rubbish!" he said when I asked him. We had met accidentally outside the warehouse of the Co-op, he strutting along, cradling his rifle and holding some new bullets which he had just that minute been to purchase. Despite the ever-present rifle, Pitseolak had not become fanatical about killing. It was more that his rifle had become an extension of himself, the tool of the trade he practised every day.

"I hear they've put them on the Eskimo Interdict List," he announced, referring to a local council decision against two men who had got drunk.

"Well, you know the rules, Pitseolak. Drunken behaviour is regarded as antisocial no matter where you are. It's a rule that covers us all — you, me, construction workers, Mounties, missionaries, the whole lot of us."

He let the butt of his rifle slip heavily and clumsily onto the trampled, hardened snow beneath his feet. "Shouldn't be any liquor up here in the first place," he unexpectedly announced, as if he was an evangelist on the brink of declaring himself to be reborn.

"Now, you're a fine one to speak about things like that," I bounced back. "I never had the chance to ask you about it before, but how come you beat up Etedlooie the other week? I thought you once told me that Eskimos weren't like that. That you don't go around hurting each other like that, and all that sort of thing."

He looked at his kamiks and I noticed that a seam was coming undone along the base of the legging. Then he shrugged his shoulders, struggling to find the right answer. "I guess you could say that that was my last fling," he remarked, puffing slightly through his nostrils. "You're right, we are not normally like that."

"But you put the gent into Frobisher hospital!"

"I know! I know what happened! And I'm really sorry that it happened. I simply got angry at him — something he said, or maybe something he did. I can't remember now. But, like I said before, it's all over now. That was my last fling." He paused and grinned mischievously. "I'm free of all of the wild, wicked ways of the kadloonas now!" Then he walked away, chuckling like some naughty little boy who had got away with it.

Apart from such brief distractions, I found that, when I was on my own, my mind was a jumbled mosaic of reflections, remembering isolated scenes like the time when a teen-ager, in a flood of adolescent fury, had challenged me: "Why are you here? Why do you make us learn your language — just so that we can speak to you? You should learn to speak our language when you come up here to our land! What is it that you kadloonas want with us? Why not leave us alone to hunt and be happy with ourselves? We can live in this land without the kadloonas, but they cannot live here without our help. This is Eskimo land. Leave us alone, in peace!"

And that was what I had decided to do.

Jill and I spent our last night with Mangitak and his family. He was a rare friend whose company and companionship I knew we would both miss greatly. I had expected to see Pitseolak at some time during the nocturnal vigil, but, as always, he was out hunting. So we sat there without him, the hours solidly ticking away as we talked, laughed, ate, and played. The children, succumbing to sleep wherever they had been sitting or lying, were sprawled in ungainly postures over the floor and in the corners. In the centre of the room, Mangitak's wife Alayaa was meticulously cutting polar bears and seals from scraps of white felt, sewing them onto a thick navy blue waistcoat which she was determined to finish so that Jill could wear it on the plane as a going-away present.

From time to time, we hacked off chunks of raw seal meat from the mound stored behind the flimsy door, chewing it enthusiastically while we flipped through hundreds of pictures recording our lives together — parties, poses, action shots, candid shots, photographs capturing funny moments or the totally unexpected. It was a night of noise and laughter, but there were moments of silence too: Mangitak pointlessly whittling the end of a plastic toothbrush which he had found lying beneath a chair by the sink; Jill picking bits of fluff from a seal skin which would be sold to the Hudson's Bay in the afternoon, after we had gone. I stood frequently by the window, looking at the snow. There were large flakes lazily descending, and whenever they landed on a nearby ledge I would inspect them closely, slowly. It was during these lulls that we all thought of the unavoidable dawning of another day, in a way hoping against hope that somehow it might never arrive. If the weather cleared, the aircraft was scheduled to land shortly after noon, but the heavily falling snow led us to believe that the flight might be delayed for several days.

As it turned out, the plane arrived right on time next day; without a wind, the continuing snow was of little threat. Fatalistically, we watched our baggage being carted aboard and then stacked into lockers as if we were going on a long-distance coach ride.

I had walked to the landing strip alone, deliberately passing the fenced enclosure which contained the tomb of Pootoogook. I paused without intending to do so. "Peace, old man," I heard myself saying, "peace." Then we were all huddled around the plane, waiting to board, saying our farewells. I saw Peter Pitseolak standing in the middle of the silent row of community elders.

"Will you come back in September?" he asked.

"No," I replied. He merely nodded and said no more. I went along the row, shaking hands, saying goodbye... Oshaweetok, Kananginak, Tytoosie, Paulassie, Simon... Saila, Jonnibo...and then I said goodbye to Mangitak and his family.

Pitseolak emerged from the rear, jogging, tired and sweaty.

"Just returned from hunting!" he half-gasped as he greeted us. "Wanted to say goodbye. Thought I'd missed you! Where's Jill? Good! Didn't want to miss you!"

A long way behind him I saw the shape of Akeeagok, sluggishly striding our way. I could see that they were both worn out.

"Where were you?" I asked Pitseolak.

"Oh, way out this time. Went beyond Tessik towards Frobisher. The herds have all but gone now. Guess it's back to seal and ducks for the next few months." He was laughing, happy, pleased with himself. Pleased that they had managed to race back and get here in time.

"Where were you when you heard the plane?" I asked.

"Oh, way back there at Peter Pitseolak's old place."

"But that's miles away!"

"Yes. We had to leave the sled there, otherwise we would not have got here in time. I'll go back for it later."

There was movement at the plane, a passenger was already going up the steps.

"Must go!" I said.

"I hope you find what you want," he said. "I am very happy now. Remember that." We shook hands and parted.

"Buy me some sausages in Marks 'n Sparks!" I heard Munarmeekudluk shouting as I clambered aboard. I peered through the window and caught a glimpse of him adjusting the brim of his celebrated hat. At his shoulder, Pitseolak offered a single wave. Then we rose into the air, and it was all gone.

Sixteen

Readjusting to life away from the Arctic wasn't as easy as I had expected it to be. Noise and perpetual movement suddenly replaced the tranquil stillness of the tundra; gaudy colours flashed before my eyes instead of subtle shades of white. There were sirens, trains, front-door bells, school children shouting as they ran along the sidewalks, people mowing lawns and having picnics in the shade of sprawling trees. And when a plane soared overhead, it didn't land on the hills nearby as I half-expected it would. It was ironic that Jill and I, rather than Pitseolak, should now be feeling like outsiders in our own world.

Pitseolak was frequently in our thoughts, and I wondered how he was getting on. I often looked at the harpoon head he had given me, and I frequently held it in my hand, this piece of his culture that he had so earnestly insisted I keep and treasure. I was fondling it the day the letter arrived from Cape Dorset. It was a chatty letter from the postmaster, filling me in on day-to-day events — the Co-op doing a brisk business, the ice breaking up. But then the news suddenly turned grey. Munarmeekudluk and some of his family had died from eating rotting seal meat — boisterous, gangling Munarmeekudluk. And Mangitak had tuberculosis and had been moved to Toronto for treatment.

I looked vacantly away from the page. Mr Munarmeekudluk? It was unreal. I recalled his parting jest about buying him some sausages from "Marks 'n Sparks" and forced the thought aside. I wasn't far from Toronto — I should go to see Mangitak. Sadly, I turned back to the chatty style of the postmaster's letter: "And, by the way, your friend Pitseolak died. Came back from a hunting trip one day as stiff as a board. Seems as if he got in the way of Akeeagok's rifle and got the back of his head blown off."

It had to be wrong — the wrong name, someone else. Oh, my god, not Pitseolak! Please, not him! Not Pitseolak! But as I read and reread the words, I knew that there was no mistake.

I was clenching my hands, and now I brought them smashing down on the table. I wanted to shout, cry, vomit — all at once. But, instead, I found I was shaking my head from side to side, muttering, "Oh, Pitseolak, what have we done to you?" I didn't really know what I meant, except that he and I were the ones called "we".

"What's wrong with you?" Jill was asking in a perky voice.

"He's dead. Pitseolak is dead," I replied, almost casually. I gave her the letter and went out for a walk.

Although tragedy was almost commonplace in the North, I wasn't an Eskimo and couldn't accept these things as easily. The families had doubtless grieved, even screamed at so many deaths in such a short while. But then Oshoochiak would have settled into an even keel once more, as would the remnants of Munarmeekudluk's family. Things would have become harshly calm again, without prolonged, overt mourning. "When we're gone, we're gone" Pitseolak had once said to me, but I hadn't accepted the simple philosophy then and couldn't now.

I sat down on the grass. It was warm, soft, gentle — the green, green grass of home, just like the popular song. Except that we, Pitseolak, Nowdluk, all of us, used to sing "the white, white snows of home."

We shouldn't have left in the first place, I was thinking. But it was an emotional reaction, for clearly there would have been nothing we could have done to prevent any of the disasters. By being there, we wouldn't have changed a thing. The only difference was that we would have been to the funerals. And at least I wouldn't be sitting here alone, without knowing how the accident had happened — without knowing why Pitseolak had died.

In my hands, I realized that I was screwing up a photograph which had come with the letter. It was glossy, black and white. It showed Pitseolak lying on the duck-boarding outside the nursing station — dying.

I have never been able to take pictures of dead people, and as I stared at the print I couldn't resist feeling how callous and unfair it had been to do this to Pitseolak. Getting him in focus. But I couldn't stop staring at it. He was wearing his windbreaker and his hair was tousled, untidy as always. One might have thought he was alseep, had it not been for the awkwardly folded arms and his rigid inflexible expression. I turned it sideways to look into his face and saw how he had just begun to respond to the initial shock and pain, the skin wrinkled at the corners of his eyes, the lips parted in readiness for a scream that never came. Yes, it was Pitseolak. And I knew now that he was dead.

I tried calling Cape Dorset on the radio-telephone but always received the recorded message: "Sorry, weather and atmospheric conditions make it impossible to connect your call. Please try another day. Thank you." So I decided to go to Toronto and see Mangitak.

We met on the steps outside the hospital. Mangitak was paler but slightly plumper, and the texture of his skin had begun to mellow in the medicated warmth of the ward. He was less rugged and even a little more casual and relaxed than normal.

I wanted to ask him about Pitseolak's death from the

first moments of our reunion but couldn't seem to get it out. Instead, we wandered round museums and art galleries, talking of other things. I finally broached the subject when we were sitting at the top of the steps which led into the Eskimo wing of the hospital. It was chilly, but hardly cold; a grey cloud had lingered overhead, threatening rain that had not yet come. Mangitak was wearing a parka that I had given him; Alayaa had made it smaller and it fitted him well. We talked of his wife and children, and of Mosesee, the daughter who had also been in the tubercular ward but had now returned to the North, cured.

"And your father?" I asked. "How is he?" It was the lead question.

"He is fine now, back at work and looking well. He is much better."

"Has he got over the accident?"

"He was very unwell at first, but now he is not unwell." Mangitak hesitated before adding, "But he is still sad."

I stared at his hands, watching his fingers stripping a broken match.

"How did it happen, Mangitak? How did Pitseolak die?"

Sadness showed briefly in his eyes as he cast his mind back to the event and its aftermath, to those hours when he lost a brother. But he spoke with a confidence that betrayed no emotion. He flicked the match into the air with force, glanced upwards at the brewing skies.

"It was a clear day," he began, "cloudless and without any snow falling. The last had come a few days before and we now expected that none would come down for the rest of the summer...." Silently, I listened to his account.

The ground had been wet, soggy, even marshlike as the snows continued to melt and the permafrost below gradually thawed to the top few inches. The snow, which had long covered the sea ice, was also beginning to melt. The period called "break up" had begun. During the daytime, massive chunks of ice would calve from the floe edge and then drift southwards, bobbing away like gigantic bits of screwed-up paper tossed into the waters by some playful child.

But always break-up time heralded more serious things for the hunters of Cape Dorset. It meant, first of all, that they would have to leave their homes during the frostiness of the pre-dawn hours, long before the surface began to melt under the omnipresent sun. But it also meant that they would now have to travel shorter distances to shoot the seal at the edge.

Pitseolak and Akeeagok set off that day before the sleeping settlement had stirred, and for miles around they were the only two moving people, the only blemishes in the Arctic stillness. Pitseolak drove the skidoo carefully, his eyes scanning the encircling whiteness, alert for the telltale lines ahead that would forewarn them of weaknesses in the ice below. Akeeagok sat behind, his head turning slowly, constantly on the lookout for animal movement — a rifle perched across his lap with deceptive casualness.

They stopped where they had left their boat the day before and found it coated with a lighter layer of soft snow, snow that had fallen during the night. Then they dragged it into the water.

Pitseolak jumped into the boat first and then Akeeagok after him, giving it a final thrust to take it clear of the edge. Pitseolak offered a couple of gentle strokes with a rough-hewn paddle, just to set them away, off into a clear direction without disturbing the waters too much. A seal bobbed its head above the surface, snorted, and descended again before either was ready to enter the hunt. They settled themselves comfortably onto their knees, positioned rifles, and were ready. The waves lapped quietly behind them, gently slapping the tender line of the floe edge as if not to disturb the silence. Then another seal bobbed its head.

"The first!" exclaimed Pitseolak, as he dispatched it with his rifle. "It will be a good day." And on they paddled.

Then suddenly Akeeagok called, "There, over there!" Pitseolak rose to look — putting his head in the line of fire just as Akeeagok pulled the trigger. The bullet hit him squarely on the back of the head.

He fell into the bottom of the boat, bleeding, dying, and Akeeagok collapsed with him, holding him, crying, screaming for help, though he knew there was no one to help him. He paddled back to shore, strapped Pitseolak to the sled behind the skidoo, and then made full-speed for the settlement.

It was a totally distraught figure that burst into the nursing station, shouting at the top of his voice. Even before the nurses reached the sled, a crowd had already gathered — old ladies wailing, hands outstretched in helpless disbelief. Then Pitseolak was carried up the steps into the nursing station and placed between the clean sheets of a narrow, metal-framed bed. Mangitak and Oshoochiak joined him there. As emergency messages to Frobisher crackled in the background, they stood helplessly beside Pitseolak, trying to understand his mumbled words.

"I knew then that nothing could be done for him," Mangitak told me, lifting his head to look at me. "When Pitseolak was on the stretcher, waiting for the plane to come, I felt he was perhaps dead already. He died on the way to the hospital in Frobisher."

We sat in silence for a while. Then I asked, "And what about Akeeagok?"

"Akeeagok didn't know what to do when he came back with my brother," said Mangitak. "He was frightened, upset. He didn't know which way to turn. We tried calming him, telling him it was not his fault, that it was an accident. But he was crying and shaking from what had happened. The nurse gave him some pills to keep him quiet, but he was just walking around, eyes wide open — scared by what he had done. My father tried to help him, to hold him by the shoulders to calm him down, but it was as if nobody could help him."

Mangitak paused, as if gently easing down from some grotesque high. The first drop of rain had blurred itself on a lower step. We watched it soak in, then disappear.

"Akeeagok was ill for many days because of what happened to my brother....But he is all right now." Mangitak shook his head slowly from side to side in reflective disbelief. Then in a clear voice, he added, "But we do not blame him. It was not his fault."

"I'm sure it wasn't," I agreed. "It sounds like a very sad accident...."

"In a way, yes. But then Pitseolak, what he did, that was not very sensible. In a way, what happened maybe was his own fault."

I frowned, stared at him, and asked, "Why? Why do you say that? Surely, it was just an accident?"

"But he moved! He moved!"

Mangitak had risen, was already turning to go inside, back to his ward, out of the rain. I turned to face him in the doorway.

"But it's natural!" I called. "If someone shouts, then it's just natural to turn and see what they are talking about." I was on my feet, standing beside him. "If I heard someone shout, right now, I'd turn my head without even thinking — just to see what it was." My head jerked as I spoke, flicking in response to some imaginary voice beckoning from beyond the shrubbery.

"An Eskimo wouldn't," Mangitak replied. "That's the whole point! A true Eskimo wouldn't move, but would stand still. He wouldn't move!"

I stood rigid, immobilized by his tone and the command of his voice. Our eyes were now fixed as one. He stared, willing me to understand something which seemed so clear to him — yet beyond me. He breathed deeply and moved a hand so that a finger tapped his temple.

"You see, that's the point! My brother just didn't *think* like an Eskimo — and so died."

There was silence.

We shook hands, parted company, and went on our ways. I have always felt that it was best that Pitseolak never heard those final words.